THE DEATH OF SOCRATES

*An Interpretation of the Platonic Dialogues:
Euthyphro, Apology, Crito and Phaedo*

by

ROMANO GUARDINI

Translated from the German
by
BASIL WRIGHTON

LONDON
SHEED & WARD
1948

INTRODUCTORY NOTE

THE FATE of Socrates is one of the principal themes in the history of the western mind. Whatever might be the paths of philosophical reflection from the year 399 B.C., they must lead back sooner or later to that enigmatic figure which so deeply touches all who come in contact with it. Socrates is not a systematic philosopher, yet he tells us more about the meaning of philosophy than many systematic writings. He is inimitable, yet he has had a deeper influence on men's minds than most others who have taught a way of life. There is in his fate, which is so completely the result of a given situation and so intimately bound up with his personal idiosyncrasy, a typical significance which scarcely any other historical figure possesses.

Not every personality admits of what is called *contact* in such a degree. This requires a character which is not simply equivalent with greatness of mind or human lovableness. A man may have admirable qualities, but of such a kind that they raise a barrier between him and those who would approach him. Another has the greatest influence, but only through his achievements, while he himself, personally, remains in the background. Again there are characters which captivate people, but are of no significance beyond that. "Contact" means the meeting with an historical figure which is unmistakably itself but yet represents something universally valid. History cannot show many such figures, which by their very unrepeatable singularity lead straight to the essential things; and among them it is perhaps Socrates who possesses in the highest degree this power of touching and moving people.'

The Socrates of the Platonic dialogues is himself the result of a contact. Thoroughly real, but as perceived and drawn by Plato—just as Plato himself is inescapably the man who lived for ten years under the influence of Socrates. It is true, there are parts of his literary work in which the two personalities fall further apart. Thus the Socrates of the earlier dialogues is nearest to the peculiar man who held himself aloof from all theory and was ever retreating into inaccessible regions; while in the *Laws*, the work of Plato's old age, the figure of Socrates is missing altogether, and the speaker is the absolutist philosopher himself with his urge towards a system. But the Socrates of the early dialogues too is the Socrates whom Plato saw and loved, and even in the latest flights of Plato's metaphysical thought the spirit of his long dead master is still active.

The reader of the Platonic dialogues is always having to stop and ask himself whether the figure who speaks under the name of Socrates really is Socrates. Often enough the answer is that it cannot be decided, but that for the most part the mind and character of the figure point back to tendencies which must, or at least might, have been found in the original Socrates. That this man, who may be regarded equally as a great sophist or as one driven by the force of Eros, as the first critical philosopher or as one guided by numinous intimations, is nevertheless a real personality of the highest potency, proves the genuine historical reality that lies behind him—and indeed also the artistic genius of the man who has drawn his portrait.

For Plato, who makes such keen demands on accuracy of thought and shows such watchful mistrust of artistic talents, is really no mere thinker, but a poet of a high order. He writes delightful scenes which betray the born dramatist, and invents thought-laden myths which interpret the meaning of life. Forms full of life and individuality move through his dialogues: the Sophists with their pretentiousness and inward emptiness; the practical men who call themselves realists and yet have to be told that they are trading in uncertainty; the poets who claim divine inspiration, and the priests who claim to be initiated, but who alike can give no rational account of their utterances; above all, the young men with their thirst for knowledge and their impetuous will for the ideal, all alike in their faith in what is new, but each with a recognizable manner of his own. In the midst of this bustling world he presents Socrates, showing his influence in all directions, and the lights that fall on his character from all sides. There is something quite peculiar to the poetic genius of Plato in his ability to make convictions grow into forces, ideas into flesh and blood. The characters of his dialogues have each an intellectual locality and definite views; but their picture is constructed from their respective standpoint and from their conviction or uncertainty.

Their relation to truth becomes itself a live figure. A dramatism of the mind sways Plato's works, and what appears as a dialectic of thought is at the same time the expression of an inward process in the thinker himself. But the point towards which and from which this living thought-process is set in motion, and this dramatism evolves, is Socrates. Plato's thought does not work from out of itself in the manner of a monologue, but springs continually from the living tensions which arise between master and disciple, between the pioneer and his opponents—as, indeed, it was awakened in himself by that contact, made at the height of his youthful receptivity, which led to many years' fellowship of life and learning. It gave him the original philosophic experience, and it recurs in the various contacts with Socrates which his dialogues describe.

Plato has built up a work of thought which can be analysed from its fundamental motives and followed in its development. We should, however, only grasp the aim of his philosophy in part if we looked for it merely in theoretical propositions. Just as urgent for him, if not more urgent, than the search for philosophic truth, is the consideration what sort of a man one must be if one is to have any prospect of finding truth. Plato has undertaken not only a critique of reason in general, but of reason in the concrete too. He is one of that quite small number of philosophers who have seen in philosophy the content of existence as well as that of propositions, and who have enquired what sort of a man one must be to become a philosopher, and what sort of a man one becomes when one has decided for philosophy. This philosophical existence he has defined theoretically—especially in the Sixth Book of the *Republic*—by laying down the gifts which the prospective philosopher must have and the formation he must receive; but he has repeatedly shown him too in the very act of philosophizing. And he has portrayed him in significant situations of life, mastering them in a way that is valid and produces knowledge: for instance, in the *Symposium*, discoursing of the highest things on a festive occasion; in the *Republic*, engaged in building up, in a spirit of deepest responsibility, that whole which is to form the synthesis of all individual achievements and at the same time the foundation which will make each particular achievement possible, namely the State; finally, in the *Euthyphro, Apology, Crito* and *Phaedo*, confronted with death and enabled by his convictions to undergo it in the right way. This philosopher however, the existential counterpart of the philosophical proposition, is no abstract construction, but the most living actuality—that very Socrates who moves to and fro throughout the Platonic dialogues. Thus what was said above of "contact" acquires a new meaning and urgency.

The present work proposes to examine four dialogues from Plato's works: the *Euthyphro, Apology, Crito* and *Phaedo*. They describe Socrates, the philosopher, in the situation of death. First he is shown, already under indictment, meeting an acquaintance in the street, outside the office of the Archon Basileus, when in the course of conversation the coming event throws its shadow before; then at the trial before the supreme court, defending his life-work against the various accusations; next in prison, at the moment when, towards the end of his imprisonment, a friend urges him to flight and he reassures himself as to his highest duty; lastly, just before the end, as he sums up, in animated conversation with his disciples, the result of his enquiries and knowledge. These texts will tell us how Socrates sees death, how his life appears to him in the face of death, and how he meets his end.

We are concerned indeed here with the theoretical proposition, what is the meaning of death, how far the possibility of death reaches into man's existence, whether there is anything indestructible in this existence, and so forth—but also with the concrete state of mind which lies behind the questions and statements; with the existence of the man who is here asking and affirming, and who is not just anyone, but Socrates; that Socrates who is the outcome of the contact between the stonemason of Alopece and his great disciple, combining in himself elements from the nature of both. This work, then, will not raise the question as to which parts of the four dialogues are historically Socratic or Platonic; the Socrates of which it speaks is that presiding genius of Plato's dialogues who has continued to influence the philosophical life of the West.

The texts mentioned are taken as a unity. It is not thereby asserted that they were planned as a unity or even composed at the same period. If Plato's work falls into four periods—youth, transition, maturity and old age—the *Phaedo* belongs to the time of mastery, while the other three dialogues are a product of the early years. With regard to the order in which the latter appeared, probably the *Apology* was written first, then the *Crito*, and last the *Euthyphro*. Our enquiry is concerned with the unity which results from the contents themselves. The *Phaedo* differs from the other dialogues in the thought as well as in the manner in which it draws the figure of Socrates; but the force of the event round which they are all grouped is so great that it prevails over the difference. And what is really the expression of Plato's intellectual and artistic growth, succeeding ever better in drawing out the potentialities of the figure, appears here as that development and transformation which occurs in Socrates in the hours before death, "when men most are wont to prophesy".

Finally, as regards the method of the enquiry: it follows the text as closely as possible, clarifying and connecting the conclusions by inserting shorter or longer recapitulations. In this way certain thoughts must keep recurring; but that is sufficiently compensated by the advantage that the theoretical considerations arise immediately from the text.

The purpose of this work is a philosophical interpretation, seeking to enter into Plato's thought; not in order to state and retrace his ideas historically, but in order to approach, under their guidance, nearer to the truth itself. Such a method must aim primarily at bringing the text itself into the greatest possible prominence.

This book—so much at least may be said—is the fruit of a real contact with the figure of Socrates. I have kept returning to the texts in the effort to grasp the thought behind Socrates's statements and the mode of existence implied by that thought. Perhaps the result does not give a ready clue to the amount of work behind it, especially as this is not indicated by the usual apparatus. This implies no depreciation of philological and historical research, for which on the contrary I have the highest respect. But it is not my line—any more than it was in earlier studies of a similar kind. The reader, then, must decide whether the view of Socrates's character and message is true enough, and the presentation of this view clear enough, to justify the book.

The translation of the Dialogues is that made by F. J. Church for his *Trial and Death of Socrates*.

CONTENTS

	PAGE
Introductory Note	v

EUTHYPHRO

Prologue
Socrates's Case	1
Euthyphro's Case	3
Socratic Irony	5
The Movement of the Dialogue	8

The Problem and its Discussion
The First Series of Questions	9
The Question concerning Essence	13
Essence and Fact	16
Piety and Justice	19
Piety and Service of the Gods	22

Conclusion 24

APOLOGY

Preface 27

The First Speech
The Spiritual Perspective	30
The Introduction	31
The Accusation of the Three	37

CONTENTS

PAGE

The Second Speech
   The Introduction 56
   The Alternative Proposal 57

The Third Speech
   The Reply to the Sentence 61
   The Reply to the True Judges 63

CRITO

Prologue 70

The Problem and its Discussion
   The Theme 74
   The Opinions of Men 75
   The Absoluteness of the Claim 77
   The Final Inference 80

Conclusion 88

PHAEDO

The Arrangement of the Dialogue 92

Introduction
   The Setting 94
   The Opening Events 96

The Main Discourse: Introductory
   The Message to Evenus and the Nature of Death . . 99
   The Theme 102

CONTENTS xiii

PAGE

The Main Discourse: First Part
   The Relativity of Birth and Death 109
   The Argument confirmed: *Anamnêsis* 115

The Main Discourse: A Doubt, and First Interlude . . 121

The Main Discourse: Second Part
   Indestructibility of the Soul 122
   The Philosophic Way of Life 127

The Main Discourse: Second Interlude
   Consternation 132
   Encouragement 138

The Main Discourse: Third Part
   The Answer to Simmias 141
   The Answer to Cebes and the Decisive Argument . . 142
   The Force of the Argument 161

The Myth concerning the Fate of Man after Death
   Meaning of the Myths 168
   The Picture of Existence 170

The Closing Scene 173

EUTHYPHRO

PROLOGUE

SOCRATES'S CASE

The first four sections of the dialogue depict the situation:

EUTHYPHRO. *What in the world are you doing here at the archon's porch, Socrates? Why have you left your haunts in the Lyceum? You surely cannot have an action before him, as I have.*

SOCRATES. *Nay, the Athenians, Euthyphro, call it a prosecution, not an action.*

EUTH. *What? Do you mean that someone is prosecuting you? I cannot believe that you are prosecuting anyone yourself.*

SOCR. *Certainly I am not.*

EUTH. *Then is someone prosecuting you?*

SOCR. *Yes.*

EUTH. *Who is he?*

SOCR. *I scarcely know him myself, Euthyphro; I think he must be some unknown young man. His name, however, is Meletus, and his deme Pitthis, if you can call to mind any Meletus of that deme,—a hook-nosed man with long hair, and rather a scanty beard.*

EUTH. *I don't know him, Socrates. But tell me, what is he prosecuting you for?*

SOCR. *What for? Not on trivial grounds, I think. It is no small thing for so young a man to have formed an opinion on such an important matter. For he, he says, knows how the young are corrupted, and who are their corruptors. He must be a wise man, who, observing my ignorance, is going to accuse me to the city, as his mother, of corrupting his friends. I think that he is the only man who begins at the right point in his political reforms: I mean whose first care is to make the young men as perfect as possible, just as a good farmer will take care of his young plants first, and, after he has done that, of the others. And so Meletus, I suppose, is first clearing us off, who, as he says, corrupt the young men as they grow up; and then, when he has done that, of course he will turn his attention to the older men, and so become a very great public benefactor. Indeed, that is only what you would expect, when he goes to work in this way.*

Two remarkable men have met, quite by accident and at a dubious place: namely in Athens, before the office building of the Second Archon, who still retains the title of *Basileus* from the time of the kings, and whose duty it is to hear indictments concerned with political crimes. One of these men is Socrates, the somewhat eccentric philosopher who is well known in the city; the other is Euthyphro, a priest and a person of no great consequence. From the very first words of the dialogue we hear that Socrates is accused; it is the first stage of the case which was tried before the supreme court in the year 399 B.C. and ended with his condemnation.

Socrates's character comes out at once in the first words: bantering and yet with deep inward concern, ironical and serious. At the same time the prosecutor is sketched. He is an unknown young man, of somewhat sorry appearance; a poet, as we shall hear later, without much substance, but with all the more arrogance, clever and with an eye to his own advantage.

To Euthyphro's question, what, according to Meletus, are Socrates's pernicious teachings, the latter replies:

> *In a way which sounds strange at first, my friend. He says that I am a maker of gods; and so he is prosecuting me, he says, for inventing new gods, and for not believing in the old ones.*

Euthyphro rejoins:

> *I understand, Socrates. It is because you say that you always have a divine sign. So he is prosecuting you for introducing novelties into religion; and he is going into court knowing that such matters are easily misrepresented to the multitude, and consequently meaning to slander you there. Why, they laugh even me to scorn, as if I were out of my mind, when I talk about divine things in the assembly, and tell them what is going to happen: and yet I have*

never foretold anything which has not come true. But they are jealous of all people like us.

Socrates, then, is accused of undermining the traditional piety. But the accusation is at once set in a strange light, both by the personality of the accuser and by the proximity into which the other speaker, Euthyphro, puts his own case with that of Socrates. For the man's very first words give the impression that he is not a first-rate character. From all these doubts, however, emerges, right from the beginning of the dialogue, that striking phenomenon which marks the religious figure of Socrates and will later, in the *Apology*, play so pathetic a rôle—his *Daimonion*. It appears that Socrates himself has never made a secret of it. It is such common knowledge among his acquaintances that even Euthyphro, who is evidently not of the inner circle, can see in it the occasion for the indictment. For whenever Socrates is about to do something that is not right—and, as will appear, this criterion of rightness extends from the foreground of the practical to the furthest depths of the existential—something warns him; often, as he says, in the middle of a sentence, so that he has to pause. He has always taken this voice very seriously. It certainly does not stand for the voice of reason or conscience, as a rationalistic interpretation would have it. Rather it is quite plainly a question of some warning coming from without and bearing a numinous character. This alone explains how Socrates's talk of his "daemonic sign" could be misinterpreted as a new religious message, endangering the traditional beliefs.

Euthyphro's Case

EUTH. *Well, Socrates, I dare say that nothing will come of it. Very likely you will be successful in your trial, and I think that I shall be in mine.*

Socrates replies with a question:

And what is this suit of yours, Euthyphro? Are you suing, or being sued?

EUTH. *I am suing.*

Socr. *Whom?*

Euth. *A man whom I am thought a maniac to be suing.*

Socr. *What? Has he wings to fly away with?*[1]

Euth. *He is far enough from flying; he is a very old man.*

Socr. *Who is he?*

Euth. *He is my father.*

Socr. *Your father, my good sir?*

Euth. *He is indeed.*

Socr. *What are you prosecuting him for? What is the charge?*

Euth. *It is a charge of murder, Socrates.*

Socrates is taken aback.

Good heavens, Euthyphro! Surely the multitude are ignorant of what makes right. I take it that it is not everyone who could rightly do what you are doing; only a man who was already well advanced in wisdom.

Euth. *That is quite true, Socrates.*

Socr. *Was the man whom your father killed a relative of yours? Nay, of course he was: you would never have prosecuted your father for the murder of a stranger?*

Euth. *You amuse me, Socrates. What difference does it make whether the murdered man was a relative or a stranger? The only question that you have to ask is, did the slayer slay justly or not? If justly, you must let him alone; if unjustly, you must indict him for murder, even though he share your hearth and sit at your table. The pollution is the same, if you associate with such a man, knowing what he has done, without purifying yourself, and him too, by bringing him to justice. In the present case the murdered man was a poor dependent of mine, who worked for us on our farm in Naxos. In a fit of drunkenness he got in a rage with one of our slaves, and killed him. My father therefore bound the man hand and foot and threw him into a ditch, while he sent to Athens to ask the seer what he should do. While the messenger was gone, he entirely neglected the man, thinking that he was a murderer, and that it would be no great matter, even if he were to die. And that was exactly what happened; hunger and cold and his bonds killed him before the messenger*

---

[1] A pun in the Greek; the word for "to prosecute", *diôkein*, means also "to pursue".

returned. And now my father and the rest of my family are indignant with me because I am prosecuting my father for the murder of this murderer. They assert that he did not kill the man at all; and they say that, even if he had killed him over and over again, the man himself was a murderer, and that I ought not to concern myself about such a person, because it is unholy for a son to prosecute his father for murder. So little, Socrates, do they know the divine law of holiness and unholiness.

In the last sentence the key-word of the dialogue has been spoken, and Socrates at once takes it up:

And do you mean to say, Euthyphro, that you think that you understand divine things, and holiness and unholiness, so accurately that, in such a case as you have stated, you can bring your father to justice without fear that you yourself may be doing an unholy deed?

EUTH. *If I did not understand all these matters accurately, Socrates, I should be of no use, and Euthyphro would not be any better than other men.*

SOCRATIC IRONY

The question, then, with which the dialogue is concerned is the nature of piety, interwoven with that of the fate of Socrates, who himself is charged with an offence against piety and religion. But in what a peculiar way the question is put! How inappropriate, one would think, to the deadly seriousness of the situation! For it is the prelude to a tragedy which, at the time of writing, must have been a matter not only of clearest recollection but of keenest feeling to the author of the dialogue. Plato was then still young, barely thirty; and Socrates was his master, who had shown him the way to all that was great; not only venerated, but loved, and taken away by an event in which the disciple can see nothing but injustice and evil. How is he to speak about it then? The answer seems undoubted: as the *Apology* speaks. Yet here is the *Euthyphro*, forming the introduction to the *Apology*—a sort of satyric drama, placed before instead of after the tragedy. This can only be because Socrates was just as this dialogue describes him. In fact he was not only the heroic philosopher depicted in the *Apology*, *Crito* and *Phaedo*. From these works alone his personality and his death would not stand out in their full character; another note is wanting, that of the *Euthyphro*. By this an air of disdain is thrown over the whole affair—though at the same time care is taken that Socrates shall remain wholly Socrates. The *Euthyphro* is, among the texts with which we are concerned, that in which the irony of Socrates appears most clearly. This peculiarity is shown in the other texts too, but it is overborne by the solemnity of the mood. In the *Euthyphro* the irony unfolds with all its effortless and redoubtable power.

What is the real meaning of it? What does a man do when he treats another with irony? He makes him ridiculous. But he could do that without irony. He could say something straight out which would put the object of his attack in a comic light; but that would not look well. It would show up the attacker as unimaginative and coarse. There is another drawback too: to attack directly shows one to be entangled in the situation, while the wielder of irony stands above it. He makes appreciative remarks, but in such a way that an unfavourable meaning appears through them. His assent only underlines the contradiction more plainly. He assumes an inoffensive air, only to wound the more surely. The ironic attack shows the aggressor in blithe security. All this could be said of irony in general; but Socratic irony is more than this. In the last resort its object is not to expose, to wound, to despatch, but to help. It has a positive aim: to stimulate movement and to liberate. It aims at serving truth. But would it not be better to teach directly, to refute, warn, challenge? Only when the truth in question can be communicated in this way. Socrates's concern is, above all things, for an inward mobility, a living relation to being and truth, which can only with difficulty be elicited by direct speech. So irony seeks to bring the centre of a man into a state of tension from which this mobility arises; either in the interlocutor himself, or, if he is not to be helped, in the listener. But how does irony gain this positive character? By the speaker's putting himself into the situation. He must not be one who lectures others in the consciousness of his own secure possession, but one who is himself a seeker. The wielder of Socratic irony is not satisfied with his own state. He knows—or at least suspects—what he ought to be, but has no illusions about the fact that he is not so. He has a keen sense for what is wrong in others, but he is just as keenly critical of himself. His superiority to his opponent lies ultimately in the fact that he is not only cleverer and more adroit, but that he does not delude himself. He "knows that he knows nothing"—not in a sceptical spirit, however, but conscious that this only obliges him to explore all the more resolutely, and with confidence that this exploration will one day lead to a real find.

So he provokes the man who is secure in his own ignorance; not in order to make a fool of him, but to stir him into movement. He accosts him thus: "What a strange thing it is that people think they know and are goodness knows what, and yet they neither know anything nor are anything. You have not found that out yet; I have. So laugh at men; but don't forget that you are a man yourself, and laugh at yourself too. The moment you can do that, your eyes are opened. Mark the difference between genuine and spurious, reality and appearance. Be exacting, not in your own interest, but in that of truth; and not against others, but against yourself. The true standard lies in yourself, and the power also of subjecting yourself to it." Thus there is in Socratic irony both a passion for the cause and a deep kindness.

One point more: it reveals a special experience of existence. Existence is powerful, splendid, fearful, mysterious and much else—but it is also odd. It is such that it excites not only the sense of great "surprise", astonishment at its height and depth, the "amazement at the essences of things", but also the twin feeling of this, the sense of the queer, contradictory, complicated. This too finds expression in irony. Irony is no less serious than direct speech, but it knows that life cannot really be grasped if one takes it too solemnly. It thinks that seriousness can itself be a kind of evasion—taking refuge in poses and phrases. The genuine ironical man is a man with a great heart and a sensitive soul; that is why he cannot endure direct statement for long. He is a lover, but round the corner, so to speak. Such was Socrates. Alcibiades puts it best when he says in the *Symposium* (215a–b) that Socrates is like one of those ugly Silenus-figures which you can open, and then golden images of the gods gleam at you from inside them. And it is a wonderful thing that Plato, himself anything but an ironical mind, but an absolutist of the purest water and tending to the doctrinaire and despotic, made this man his master.

The first of the four dialogues which extol the greatness of Socrates gives freest play to his irony.

The Movement of the Dialogue

It is as though Euthyphro states the theme of the dialogue—the human theme behind the intellectual; the passionate emotion of the spirit called forth by the dialogue behind the logical effort—when he says in the eleventh section:

But, Socrates, I really don't know how to explain to you what is in my mind. Whatever we put forward always somehow moves round in a circle, and will not stay where we place it.

Towards the end of the dialogue Socrates himself—and with what delightful satire—takes up the statement and confirms it:

After that, shall you be surprised to find that your definitions move about, instead of staying where you place them? Shall you charge me with being the Daedalus that makes them move, when you yourself are far more skilful than Daedalus was, and make them go round in a circle? Do you not see that our definition has come round to where it was before?

In this circular movement something vital is happening. At the beginning Euthyphro brings himself into dangerous proximity with Socrates, as a specialist, so to speak, in prophecy and religious science addressing a colleague. This association then gets involved in the vortex of the irony, and neatly decomposed, as by a centrifugal force of the mind, into its elements. In the end, indeed, neither Socrates nor Euthyphro is defined, philosophically or even psychologically; but their difference has come into view and they can no longer be confused. The intellectual point, too, remains undefined. The question, what *is* true piety, has been given no answer; but it has become clear that at any rate it has nothing to do with what Euthyphro means and is. And Socrates's words have revealed hidden depths, so that the reader sees how the question about the essence of piety ought to be attacked.

Besides this, however, the reader has become aware of something else: namely, that Socrates's accusers—as also a large proportion of his judges — are people of Euthyphro's stamp. The latter is well disposed to Socrates. But if Socrates cannot make himself comprehensible even to Euthyphro, how will he be able to do so to people of the same kind who also hate him? Euthyphro himself would know how to dispose of such adversaries. One believes him at once when he says:

> *Yes, by Zeus, Socrates, I think I should find out his weak points, if he were to try to indict me. I should have a good deal to say about him in court long before I spoke about myself.*

In such a contest like would be matched with like. But Socrates will neither have the weapons necessary for the coming contest, nor, if he had them, would he know how to use them. So from the dialogue, conducted almost with arrogance on Socrates's part, comes a breath of tragic presentiment of what is to follow.

THE PROBLEM AND ITS DISCUSSION

THE FIRST SERIES OF QUESTIONS

Socrates then begins, stating the theme of the dialogue:

> *Now, therefore, please explain to me what you were so confident just now that you knew. Tell me what are piety and impiety with reference to murder and everything else.*

Continuing, he brings out sharply the main Socratic-Platonic interest, the strictly philosophical question:

> *I suppose that holiness is the same in all actions; and that unholiness is always the opposite of holiness, and like itself, and that as unholiness, it always has the same essential nature, which will be found in whatever is unholy.*

Euthyphro assents, and the irony is brought to bear again; then Socrates asks further:

> *Tell me, then; what is holiness, and what is unholiness?*

The answer is one that he can hardly hear without a chuckle of delight:

> Well, then, I say that holiness means prosecuting the wrongdoer who has committed murder or sacrilege, or any other such crime, as I am doing now, whether he be your father or your mother or whoever he may be; and I say that unholiness means not prosecuting him.

The proof is equally gratifying:

> And observe, Socrates, I will give you a clear proof, which I have already given to others, that it is so, and that doing right means not suffering the sacrilegious man, whosoever he may be. Men hold Zeus to be the best and the justest of the gods; and they admit that Zeus bound his own father, Cronos, for devouring his children wickedly; and that Cronos in his turn castrated his father for similar reasons. And yet these same men are angry with me because I proceed against my father for doing wrong. So, you see, they say one thing in the case of the gods and quite another in mine.

In Socrates's rejoinder jest and earnest are curiously mingled:

> Is that not why I am being prosecuted, Euthyphro? I mean, because I am displeased when I hear people say such things about the gods? I expect that I shall be called a sinner, because I doubt those stories.[1] Now if you, who understand all these matters so well, agree in holding all those tales true, then I suppose that I must needs give way. What could I say when I admit myself that I know nothing about them? But tell me, in the name of friendship, do you really believe that these things have actually happened?

The answer which Euthyphro gives to Socrates's philosophical question is the mythical answer—more accurately, that mythical answer which in the course of historical evolution has lost its proper meaning. To be a real answer, it presupposes a certain view of man and religion with its particular type of life-experience. For this view reality is at once foreground and background. It consists not of scientifically transparent systems of matter and energy, but of forces of a natural and at the same time numinous order, which conflict mutually, and from whose incessant conflict life continually emerges.

[1] Cf. *Rep.* ii, 377, seq.

The mythical truth lies in the fact that these forces and their relation to one another reveal themselves to the onlooker in valid forms and processes. The images, therefore, by which this is done are something different from the irresponsible shapes of later, aesthetically emancipated art. They are the immediate expression of essential truth; and the man who knows about them and is familiar with them lives in the existential order. The mythical attitude implies further that the man has not yet come to dissociate himself by critical judgment and technical skill from those forces, but is still directly controlled by them. He has a constant perception of their working, not only in the constellations, in the atmospheric processes, in the rhythms of growth, but also in his own being. They determine his instinctive life, regulate the emotions and passions of his mind, and show themselves in dreams and inspirations. His fate is ever their work; the order of family and community life results from their operation and at the same time affords a protection against their tyranny.

As long as all this holds good, piety means indeed a revering gaze, a respectful self-surrender, a constant interpretation of one's own life, as of the surrounding world, in accordance with those figures and legends which have been received from experiences of past seers and handed down by religious tradition; and the question what is true and not true in a religious sense, what is right and wrong, really is answered by referring to the figure of a god or the deed of a hero. All this has as yet nothing to do with philosophy. But in the course of history the mental make-up which produces it gradually dissolves. The ideas of the Ionian philosophy of nature in some respects mark the critical point. The "Water" of Thales, the "Formless Infinite" of Anaximander, the "Air" of Anaximenes, the "Fire" of Heraclitus, are certainly not yet philosophical concepts in the proper sense, only images for the primal reality; but in them a new relation to the world already emerges. Man begins to detach himself from the ensemble of powers which have been hitherto a direct experience, wholly containing him; he begins to perceive reality differently and to examine it in a new way, the scientific and critical way. He not only contemplates phenomena, but tries to get behind them. He not only investigates the meaning of valid images, but becomes aware of the coherence of cause and effect, whole and part, means and end, and feels himself challenged to give a rational explanation. He sees himself no longer as involved in a mysterious play of natural and divine powers, which according to their particular nature have to be averted or directed by ceremonial and magical rites and precautions; he begins to see the things around him as natural objects, and to acquire and use them according to their actual qualities. So the traditional picture of the world loses its original character. Men continue to live in it, but without being deeply committed to it. Criticism grows; and as it has not yet acquired its appropriate standards, it has a largely arbitrary and destructive character. At this point stands Socrates. Men have inwardly abandoned the system of myth, even though its beautiful and venerable images still accompany them through life. Mythical thought has lost its real justification, and Euthyphro is the expression, albeit caricatured, of the actual state of things. A step forward must now be taken. The forces which have destroyed the myths must find a new norm and guarantee for life. This is done by Socrates's question: "What is the nature of things? What is the right order of existence which results from it? What are the values which give to human existence its meaning?" This question, however, is taken amiss by those circles of his native city whose spokesman is Meletus. They have no longer any real belief in the myths; but they shrink from the convulsions and labours of the break-up, and turn against the man who is bringing it about. Euthyphro, in spite of all momentary opposition, thinks as they do. His quarrel with them is conducted within an identity of views. So in his person the accusation itself becomes ludicrous.

Yes, and stranger ones, too, Socrates, which the multitude do not know of.

SOCR. *Then you really believe that there is war among the gods, and bitter hatreds, and battles, such as the poets tell of, and which the great painters have depicted in our temples, especially in the pictures which cover the robe that is carried up to the Acropolis at the great Panathenaic festival. Are we to say that these things are true, Euthyphro?*

EUTH. *Yes, Socrates, and more besides. As I was saying, I will* relate to you many other stories about divine matters, if you like, which I am sure will astonish you when you hear them.

SOCR. *I dare say.*

THE QUESTION CONCERNING ESSENCE

The first round is over, without Euthyphro's having noticed anything. Only the invisible listener has taken note, to wit, the youth of Athens, which loves Socrates, and has been listening while the whole scene is enacted. Then the master begins anew:

You shall relate them to me at your leisure another time. At present please try to give a more definite answer to the question which I asked you just now. What I asked you, my friend, was, What is holiness? and you have not explained it to me, to my satisfaction. You only tell me that what you are doing now, namely prosecuting your father for murder, is a holy act.

Euthyphro confirms this. Whereupon Socrates:

Very likely. But many other actions are holy, are they not, Euthyphro?

EUTH. *Certainly.*

SOCR. *Remember, then, that I did not ask you to tell me one or two of all the many holy actions that there are; I want to know what is the essential form of holiness which makes all holy actions holy. You said, I think, that there is one form*[1] *which makes all holy actions holy, and another form which makes all unholy actions unholy. Do you not remember?*

EUTH. *I do.*

SOCR. *Well, then, explain to me what is this form, that I may have it to turn to, and to use as a standard whereby to judge your actions, and those of other men, and be able to say that whatever action resembles it is holy, and whatever does not, is not holy.*

Here then is the question concerning essence again.

Euthyphro tries to answer:

[1] *Eidos* ("essential image") and *idea* ("original form") mean the same thing, although with a somewhat different nuance; the necessary content of a thing's property and meaning, though not by way of abstract definition, but of course

Well then, what is pleasing to the gods is holy; and what is not pleasing to them is unholy.

SOCR. *Beautiful, Euthyphro. Now you have given me the answer that I wanted. Whether what you say is true, I do not know yet. But of course you will go on to prove the truth of it.*

The answer is in fact better than the preceding one, for at least it ventures into the region of conceptual definition. But is the standard assigned, according to which the pious is what the gods love, really the right one? A standard must be unequivocal: that is, in this case, all the gods must love and hate the same things. But do they? Evidently not, for the myths are always describing their quarrels. And you cannot have a real quarrel about mere facts—for instance, whether a thing is bigger or smaller than another thing—for then one would simply measure them and the matter would be settled. It must be about matters of principle—what, for example, the just or the unjust, the beautiful or the ugly, is in itself. So if even gods quarrel, it is only about such things that they can quarrel:

SOCR. *And each of them loves what he thinks honourable, and good, and right, and hates the opposite, does he not?*
EUTH. *Certainly.*
SOCR. *But you say that the same action is held by some of them to be right, and by others to be wrong; and that then they dispute about it, and so quarrel and fight among themselves. Is it not so?*
EUTH. *Yes.*
SOCR. *Then the same thing is hated by the gods and loved by them; and the same thing will be displeasing and pleasing to them.*
EUTH. *Apparently.*
SOCR. *Then, according to your account, the same thing will be holy and unholy.*
EUTH. *So it seems.*

So this definition of piety will not do either, since it proceeds not from definable quantities, but from an uncriticized popular belief which is in fact decaying. The question of the real significance of

---

pictorial perceptibility. This "image" acquires in the course of Platonic thought an ever more pronounced metaphysical significance. See p. 150 below.

the mythical strife is not raised. When in the fight for Troy Hera is ranged against Aphrodite, the former goddess pronounces Paris's act to be reprehensible, the latter noble. This has a quite different significance from a discussion between two philosophers on ethical problems; for Aphrodite is the nature-force of love and Hera the social force of family order, both being understood not as logical principles, but as empirical and at the same time numinous life-forces. Formulated in theoretical assertions, their claims exclude one another; contradictory propositions cannot be simultaneously true. It is different in the mythical sphere. Myth says: Everything is divine. All is resolved in the unity of the world, which is itself the ultimate Divine and comprises all contradictories. So both are right, and the conflict between them is right too. Paris as well as Menelaus is under the protection of a divine power. The fact that they must fight constitutes the inevitable tragedy, in which however life does not disintegrate, but persists as a supra-intelligible whole. All this the mythically perceptive man, whose decadent phase is represented by Euthyphro, would not indeed state conceptually, but would see, feel and live. That Euthyphro's place is not taken by the real representative of myth, who, at once bound and sustained by its power, embodied it convincingly by his whole being, of course constitutes the latent injustice of the dialogue and of the Socratic-Platonic campaign against antiquity. Nevertheless the attackers are in the right, for the object of their attack is no longer the living mythical mentality, but one which has gone fundamentally astray in itself and only continues to exist by virtue of the inertia of what has once been historical fact. Thus it is, from an historical point of view, ripe for dissolution—quite apart from the fact that it is erroneous in itself;—and it must be allowable to say this, in spite of romantic considerations. The mythical order has a great power, and there is a glory over it for which the modern man, tormented with criticism, feels full of longing. But it presupposes a confusion in nature which a man cannot acquiesce in without shirking his mission. As soon as his conscience becomes aware of the self's personal value and is prepared to answer for it, he must throw off the mythical mentality. Socrates, then, is not only the advocate of what is historically ripe, but of what has a higher significance too. It is also true that in bringing forward this new and higher good he destroys much that is old and excellent, and this justifies the resistance to him. As always in historical matters, in which there is no absolute progress, he is at fault by reason of his very mission.

Essence and Fact

The attempt has miscarried again, and Socrates does not fail to bring this to his companion's notice:

> *Then, my good friend, you have not answered my question. I did not ask you to tell me what action is both holy and unholy; but it seems that whatever is pleasing to the gods is also displeasing to them. And so, Euthyphro, I should not wonder if what you are doing now in chastising your father is a deed well-pleasing to Zeus, but hateful to Cronos and Ouranos, and acceptable to Hephaestus, but hateful to Hêrê; and if any of the other gods disagree about it, pleasing to some of them, and displeasing to others.*

Euthyphro tries once more to save his thesis:

> *But on this point, Socrates, I think that there is no difference of opinion among the gods; they all hold that if one man kills another wrongfully, he must be punished.*

So far, so good; he points to the evident principle that every injustice must be atoned for. Socrates too agrees with this; nay, he elucidates the statement further in these words:

> *Then they do not dispute the proposition, that the wrongdoer must be punished. They dispute about the question, who is a wrongdoer, and when, and what is a wrong deed, do they not?*

The principle is clear, only the fact is in dispute. But what does this imply for the question under discussion? The proposition, "Injustice must be punished", amounts after all to the same as, "Injustice is unjust". But what *is* injustice? How does one distinguish a case of injustice from one of justice? Socrates formulates the question by going back to the case that is occupying their attention:

> *Come then, my dear Euthyphro, please enlighten me on this point. What proof have you that all the gods think that a labourer*

who has been imprisoned for murder by the master of the man whom
he has murdered, and who dies from his imprisonment before the
master has had time to learn from the seers what he should do,
dies by injustice? How do you know that it is right for a son to
indict his father, and to prosecute him for the murder of such a man?
Come, see if you can make it clear to me that the gods necessarily
agree in thinking that this action of yours is right. . . .*

Euthyphro evades the question—understandably, from his way of
thinking, for it again approaches the critical point. Socrates at once
makes this clear:

*. . . Suppose that Euthyphro were to prove to me as clearly as
possible that all the gods think such a death unjust; how has he brought
me any nearer to understanding what holiness and unholiness are?*

He would have to say

*. . . that whatever all the gods hate is unholy, and whatever they
all love is holy: while whatever some of them love, and others hate,
is either both or neither? Do you wish us now to define holiness and
unholiness in this manner?*

EUTH. *Why not, Socrates?*

SOCR. *There is no reason why I should not, Euthyphro. It is
for you to consider whether that definition will help you to instruct
me as you promised.*

EUTH. *Well, I should say that holiness is what all the gods love,
and that unholiness is what they all hate.*

Euthyphro has maintained that the goodness of the good consists
in its affirmation by the gods: that is, he has made a formal content
depend on the attitude taken towards something by certain beings,
even though beings of the highest order—the gods. To put it more
pointedly, he has founded an absolute principle on a fact, whereas
on the contrary the fact should be founded on the principle, which
rests on itself and cannot be proved, but only indicated.

Socrates indeed brings this home to him by asking:

*We shall know that better in a little while, my good friend.
Now consider this question. Do the gods love holiness because it is
holy, or is it holy because they love it?*

18 THE DEATH OF SOCRATES

The question here touches the decisive point, but it thereby passes beyond Euthyphro's power of comprehension. So Socrates tries to make clear to him the difference between the two propositions. The proposition, "This is pious", is a statement of essence; the proposition, "This is loved", is a statement of fact. The sense only comes out correctly when one says:

> Then it is loved by the gods because it is holy: it is not holy because it is loved by them?
> EUTH. *It seems so.*
> SOCR. *But then what is pleasing to the gods is pleasing to them, and is in a state of being loved by them, because they love it?*
> EUTH. *Of course.*
> SOCR. *Then holiness is not what is pleasing to the gods, and what is pleasing to the gods is not holy, as you say, Euthyphro. They are different things.*
> EUTH. *And why, Socrates?*
> SOCR. *Because we are agreed that the gods love holiness because it is holy; and that it is not holy because they love it. Is not this so?*
> EUTH. *Yes.*

Euthyphro has first answered "It seems so", next "Of course", then "And why, Socrates?"—and now he says "Yes". But all this only amounts to "I haven't understood a thing". And when Socrates then proceeds to draw out the relations of "pious" and "loved" in a rapid succession of statements, and asks:

> *Do not, if you please, keep from me what holiness is; begin again and tell me that. Never mind whether the gods love it, or whether it has other attributes: we shall not differ on that point. Do your best to make clear to me what is holiness and what is unholiness.*

——the poor man is quite dizzy:

> EUTH. *But, Socrates, I really don't know how to explain to you what is in my mind. Whatever we put forward always somehow moves round in a circle, and will not stay where we place it.*

And we feel the power of the master of irony when he goes on to remark:

> *I think that your definitions, Euthyphro, are worthy of my ancestor Daedalus. If they had been mine and I had laid them down, I daresay that you would have made fun of me, and said that it was the consequence of my descent from Daedalus that the definitions which I construct run away, as his statues used to, and will not stay where they are placed. But, as it is, the definitions are yours, and the jest would have no point. You yourself see that they will not stay still.*
>
> EUTH. *Nay, Socrates, I think that the jest is very much in point. It is not my fault that the definition moves round in a circle and will not stay still. But you are the Daedalus, I think: as far as I am concerned, my definitions would have stayed quiet enough.*
>
> SOCR. *Then, my friend, I must be a more skilful artist than Daedalus: he only used to make his own works move; whereas I, you see, can make other people's works move too. And the beauty of it is that I am wise against my will. I would rather that our definitions had remained firm and immovable than have all the wisdom of Daedalus and all the riches of Tantalus to boot.*[1]

PIETY AND JUSTICE

Socrates starts again, spurring on poor Euthyphro, who would certainly rather be left in peace:

> *Well, then, is all justice holy too? Or, while all holiness is just, is a part only of justice holy, and the rest of it something else?*
>
> EUTH. *I do not follow you, Socrates.*
>
> SOCR. *Yet you have the advantage over me in your youth no less than in your wisdom. But, as I say, the wealth of your wisdom makes you indolent. Exert yourself, my good friend: I am not asking you a difficult question.*

And he then works out an example by means of a poetic quotation. The two phenomena "fear" and "shame" have a different extension. The first is more general and includes the second. It is the same with

---

[1] Tantalus in Hades was surrounded by cool water and fine fruits; but whenever he tried to drink, the water dried up, and whenever he reached for the fruits, a storm-wind lifted the branches high in the air.

piety and justice. The latter—taken in the sense of natural justice or natural suitability—has a wider extension than piety. The pious forms a part of the just; it is natural suitability under a special aspect. Then he asks:

> *Then see if you can explain to me what part of justice is holiness, that I may tell Meletus that now that I have learnt perfectly from you what actions are pious and holy, and what are not, he must give up prosecuting me unjustly for impiety.*

Socrates, then, has told his companion what are the elements of a correctly constructed definition: the more general major term, and the specific difference by which the thing to be defined is classed under the former. According to this scheme Euthyphro has now to say how piety is related to justice, and so to define it.

> EUTH. *Well then, Socrates, I should say that piety and holiness are that part of justice which has to do with the attention which is due to the gods: and that what has to do with the attention which is due to men, is the remaining part of justice.*

Once more the thought has lost its elevation. Euthyphro's answer is not on Socrates's level, but has sunk to that of everyday practice. So Socrates tries to regain the higher level:

> *And I think that your answer is a good one, Euthyphro. But there is one little point, of which I still want to hear more. I do not yet understand what the attention or care which you are speaking of is. I suppose you do not mean that the care which we show to the gods is like the care which we show to other things. We say, for instance, do we not, that not everyone knows how to take care of horses, but only the trainer of horses? . . . Well, then, has not all care the same object? Is it not for the good and benefit of that on which it is bestowed? for instance, you see horses are benefited and improved when they are cared for by the art which is concerned with them. Is it not so? . . . Then is holiness, which is the care which we bestow on the gods, intended to benefit the gods, or to improve them? Should you allow that you make any of the gods better, when you do a holy action?*

EUTH. *No indeed: certainly not.*

SOCR. *No: I am quite sure that that is not your meaning, Euthyphro: it was for that reason that I asked you what you meant by the attention due to the gods. I thought that you did not mean that.*

EUTH. *You were right, Socrates. I do not mean that.*

SOCR. *Good. Then what sort of attention to the gods will holiness be?*

EUTH. *The attention, Socrates, of slaves to their masters.*

SOCR. *I understand: then it is a kind of service to the gods?*

The answer has got stuck in the practical again. The nature of the thing meant has not come out yet. What is the meaning of this "care" and this "service"?

SOCR. *Then tell me, my excellent friend; what result will the art which serves the gods serve to produce? You must know, seeing that you say that you know more about divine things than any other man.*

The train of thought has come back again—somewhat deviously—to the critical point. Euthyphro has now to say what constitutes the special significance of an act of piety. He will thereby enunciate the essence of piety and clear the way for the further question as to the essence of its superior virtue, justice. "Justice" is for Plato something ultimate and comprehensive, namely the will and ability to give everything what is due to its proper nature—therefore, rightly understood, morality as such. Euthyphro, however, does not understand what it is all about, but again talks round the point, until, pressed by Socrates, he finally declares:

I told you just now, Socrates, that it is not so easy to learn the exact truth in all these matters. However, broadly I say this: if any man knows that his words and deeds in prayer and sacrifice are acceptable to the gods, that is what is holy: that preserves the common weal, as it does private households, from evil; but the opposite of what is acceptable to the gods is impious, and this it is that brings ruin and destruction on all things.

Another disappointment. The answer begs the question. That disposition is called "pious" in which the right "service" is rendered, whereas the very thing to be determined is, in what consists the service that is right for the gods, that is, pious. At the same time the answer slips down from the region of serious thinking into that of practice—and a very dubious practice, as will soon appear.

Piety and Service of the Gods

But Socrates does not let go:

> *But you are evidently not anxious to instruct me: just now, when you were just on the point of telling me what I want to know, you stopped short. If you had gone on then, I should have learnt from you clearly enough by this time what is holiness. But now I am asking you questions, and must follow wherever you lead me; so tell me, what is it that you mean by the holy and holiness? Do you not mean a science of prayer and sacrifice?*

Apparently an attempt to come to a definition—but an insidious one, as will be seen in a moment:

> Socr. *To sacrifice is to give to the gods, and to pray is to ask of them, is it not?*
> Euth. *It is, Socrates.*
> Socr. *Then you say that holiness is the science of asking of the gods, and giving to them?*
> Euth. *You understand my meaning exactly, Socrates.*
> Socr. *Yes, for I am eager to share your wisdom, Euthyphro, and so I am all attention: nothing that you say will fall to the ground. But tell me, what is this service of the gods? You say it is to ask of them, and to give to them?*
> Euth. *I do.*
> Socr. *Then, to ask rightly will be to ask of them what we stand in need of from them, will it not?*
> Euth. *Naturally.*
> Socr. *And to give rightly will be to give back to them what they stand in need of from us? It would not be very clever to make a present to a man of something that he has no need of.*

EUTH. *True, Socrates.*

SOCR. *Then, holiness, Euthyphro, will be an art of traffic between gods and men?*

Euthyphro feels that this is questionable, and would like to let it rest there:

Yes, if you like to call it so.

But Socrates holds him fast:

Nay, I like nothing but what is true.

And he then exposes the reason for the evidently dubious character of the statement, namely the false religious ideas on which Euthyphro's argument rests.

But tell me, how are the gods benefited by the gifts which they receive from us? What they give us is plain enough. Every good thing that we have is their gift. But how are they benefited by what we give them? Have we the advantage over them in this traffic so much that we receive from them all the good things we possess and give them nothing in return?

Euthyphro sees where the ideas he has expressed are leading:

But do you suppose, Socrates, that the gods are benefited by the gifts which they receive from us?

But Socrates will not let him escape the consequences of his assertions:

But what are these gifts, Euthyphro, that we give the gods?

Euthyphro answers:

What do you think but honour, and homage, and, as I have said, what is acceptable to them.

Socrates now proceeds to close the circle:

Then holiness, Euthyphro, is acceptable to the gods, but it is not profitable, or dear to them?

EUTH. *I think that nothing is dearer to them.*
SOCR. *Then I see that holiness means that which is dear to the gods.*
EUTH. *Most certainly.*

CONCLUSION

Socr. *After that, shall you be surprised to find that your definitions move about, instead of staying where you place them? Shall you charge me with being the Daedalus that makes them move, when you yourself are far more skilful than Daedalus was, and make them go round in a circle? Do you not see that our definition has come round to where it was before? Surely you remember that we have already seen that holiness, and what is pleasing to the gods, are quite different things. Do you not remember?*

Euth. *I do.*

Socr. *And now do you not see that you say that what the gods love is holy? But does not what the gods love come to the same thing as what is pleasing to the gods?*

Euth. *Certainly.*

Socr. *Then either our former conclusion was wrong, or, if that was right, we are wrong now.*

Euth. *So it seems.*

What, then, is the outcome of the whole discussion? Substantially, nothing at all. Euthyphro has stuck to his first opinion. But could not Socrates have told him what piety really is? To such a question the master of irony would probably have answered: "But I don't know that myself!" Yet the answer might have had several meanings. It might have meant: "I know a few things, but would like to find out more. That can only happen when the other man joins in the search, therefore I cannot give away the solution to him." But perhaps the answer would have meant the following: "I cannot tell him the solution so simply as that. For either he would not understand it at all, and then it would be no use telling him. Or he would understand it as a positive statement, without perceiving the problem. He would swallow the answer and think he had got the gist of it, and then he would be a lost man as far as real knowledge goes. For only the man who is inwardly set in motion grasps the truth. So far he has not got moving, but has probably only been thinking that Socrates is a queer old gentleman who can be very importunate; and telling him the definition of piety would not get him any further than that."

The only alternative, then, is either to leave the man alone or to start again from the beginning; and the elderly questioner in facts begins afresh. To be sure, it is an odd sort of interrogation, and a dangerous undertone is audible in it:

> SOCR. *Then we must begin again, and inquire what is holiness. I do not mean to give in until I have found out. Do not deem me unworthy; give your whole mind to the question, and this time tell me the truth. For if any one knows it, it is you; and you are a Proteus whom I must not let go until you have told me. It cannot be that you would ever have undertaken to prosecute your aged father for the murder of a labouring man unless you had known exactly what is holiness and unholiness. You would have feared to risk the anger of the gods, in case you should be doing wrong, and you would have been afraid of what men would say. But now I am sure that you think that you know exactly what is holiness and what is not: so tell me, my excellent Euthyphro, and do not conceal from me what you hold it to be.*

The discussion is back at the beginning again. The domestic affair which has brought Euthyphro here crops up again; once more his competence in religious matters is emphasized, and Socrates craves instruction on the nature of piety, so that he, a man under accusation of impiety, may learn wherein he has been at fault. But Euthyphro must have felt sure of one thing: what is aimed at him here is no mere question, but an exposure and a verdict. So he takes to flight:

> EUTH. *Another time, then, Socrates. I am in a hurry now, and it is time for me to be off.*
> SOCR. *What are you doing, my friend! Will you go away and destroy all my hopes of learning from you what is holy and what is not, and so of escaping Meletus? I meant to explain to him that now Euthyphro has made me wise about divine things, and that I no longer in my ignorance speak rashly about them or introduce novelties in them; and then I was going to promise him to live a better life for the future.*

But Euthyphro is not going to let himself in for any more. One can see him hurrying away and Socrates looking after him with a smile.

The conversation has been fruitless. Euthyphro has not opened out. Even the indirect method has not succeeded in getting at him. But one thing has become clear: what he is, and what Socrates is—those two who at the beginning of the dialogue seemed so near to each other. And as Euthyphro is, so will be the majority of the judges before whom Socrates has to defend his case.

THE APOLOGY

PREFACE

THE HUMAN and intellectual situation of the *Apology* cannot be rightly understood without considering the historical and political situation. The trial of Socrates took place in 339 B.C. The years from 431 till 404 had been taken up with the Peloponnesian War, waged between Athens and Sparta for supremacy in Greece, and ending with the defeat of Athens. The war was really decided in 413 by the collapse of the Sicilian expedition. It is true that Athens won the naval battle of Arginusae as late as 406; but the commanders had been prevented by storm from burying the bodies that were drifting in the sea, and the people, overheated by religious excitement, adjudged this a crime on their part and condemned them to death. This incident reveals the inward confusion of minds. In 405 followed the final defeat at Aegospotami, and Athens was invested. In 404 the city, exhausted and torn by party strife, was compelled to surrender. The democratic constitution was abolished and authority transferred to the "Thirty Tyrants", Athenians with Spartan leanings. These men governed with moderation at first, then, supported by Spartan troops, ever more arbitrarily, and finally with violence and terror. From the frontier fortress of Phyle began a resistance movement against them which ended with the fall of the Thirty, and Sparta allowed the old form of government to be restored. The city began to recover; but the political situation was tense, as the ruling democracy felt itself threatened. So it was easy for a trend of thought which was in itself of purely intellectual purport to be misunderstood politically and felt as dangerous.

The moral and religious situation too was difficult. The endless wars with their dreadful defeats had brought in their train a deep-seated disorder. The extremely rapid and intensive development of intellectual life had shaken the traditional religious ideas. The old faith in myth and cult had, as we have already seen, been critically undermined by the versatile Athenian intellect; but equally so by a frame of mind which after all the late calamities clung only to tangible things and admitted nothing beyond success and enjoyment. Sophistry and the cult of success thus conspired to produce a religious disorder along with the ethical. And as religious life was bound up in the closest way with the life of the state, as indeed the institutions of state and society had their roots in religion, it was necessarily the interest of a democracy of conservative tendency—democracy in a different sense, therefore, from that which the modern age associates with the word—to preserve as far as possible the traditional piety. Thus, according as the situation actually stood, an attack on religious tradition could appear as an attack on the state.

Socrates had a peculiar position in relation to all this. He was only partially adjusted to the social and political mentality of the time; to the relation of man with men and things, life and work; to the prevailing piety and morality. The institutions themselves, especially those of the state, he upheld from insight and conviction as well as from solidarity of feeling—the *Crito* speaks of this with an unaffected pathos. He fulfilled his duties as a citizen, in office as in arms, in the most conscientious manner; of this too the *Crito*, as well as the *Apology*, speaks. Religious usages were sacred to him; see the end of the *Phaedo*. He certainly took part in everything that went on in the city. Countless people knew him and, according to their several characters, respected, feared, hated or laughed at him. But in that which was his very own, his mission and his inner compulsion, he was still quite alone. What he was and did in that regard had no place in the existing order of things. In fact he bore within him a power which must disrupt this whole beautiful life that rested on the forces of nature-religion and expressed itself in tradition, prophecy, myth, poetry, symbol and cult. In face of everything which claimed validity he raised the testing question: "What is this? What does it amount to? Is it fundamentally in order?" He thereby loosened just what was the strongest hold of tradition, its rootedness in involuntary feeling, judgment and action. The import of his attack was: "You claim to be acting rightly. But one can only act rightly from insight. Therefore you claim to have insight, or at any rate you act as if you had it. Give an account of it then!" But the result in every case is: "You have no real insight after all, but only opinions which derive from impulse and custom, and your action has neither sense nor justification." In all this there appears a new standard of validity and a new ethos determined by it. Instinct, the authenticity of the established order of things, the authority of tradition, the power of irrational religious experiences and the wisdom of symbols lose their reassuring and binding force. They are opposed by the capacity for personal responsibility, resting on insight into the nature of things and the duty of objectivity—an attitude, therefore, which is based on a mind become aware of itself and master of itself.

Because Socrates did this, the Athenians indicted him—the contemporary Athenians that is, combined democrats and conservatives, enemies of all despotism, but also of everything that would then have been called "modern", namely rational criticism and the shaping of life by insight and responsible planning. And according to the values on which the judgment is based, these men appear either as narrow-minded opponents of what history demanded, bent on arresting it, and even in this serving its purpose by raising the object of their attack to the position of a shining example— or as the protectors, limited perhaps, but guided by instinctive knowledge, of a splendid, threatened world, and justified by the fact that the progress of history would reveal Socrates as the man who introduced the age of rationalism and "decadence".

This is what was meant by saying that Socrates was alone in what was specially characteristic of him, a lonely man who did not fit into the institutions of his time. He was formally indicted by three men, who are mentioned in the *Apology* itself. The first was Meletus, a poet by profession, but without further significance; the second was Anytus, a rich master-tanner, a politically influential democrat and inexorable opponent of all new movements; the third was Lycon, an orator, and representative of the politicians and intellectuals. But these three men really stood for all those whose concern it was that tradition should be upheld.

One further remark on the course of the trial, the order of which stands out clearly in the action of the *Apology*.

The court is the supreme court of the state, consisting of five hundred jurors appointed by lot. First the indictment is read to it, by the prosecutor if there is only one, by a spokesman if several persons have made the accusation. In Socrates's trial there are three, and Meletus speaks for them. The accused is then given the word to begin his defence. He may set forth his view of the case, and try to refute the speaker for the prosecution by cross-questioning. When he has finished, the jurors decide whether he is guilty or not guilty in the sense of the accusation. If he is pronounced guilty, the accused has leave to speak again. The indictment has also proposed a certain penalty; the accused on his side may now name an alternative penalty which seems reasonable to him, and thus has the opportunity of a second, limited defence. The court then passes the second judgment. If it rejects the accused's proposal, the latter is allowed a final word.

Plato's work consists of the three speeches which Socrates made at the prescribed stages in the trial. To what extent these speeches correspond to Socrates's actual words cannot be determined. In any case it can be assumed that they reproduce the sense and spirit of his defence. The first speech is long, about eight times as long as the second, and interspersed with questions to the speaker for the prosecution and his answers; the second is very short; the third again about twice as long as the second.

THE FIRST SPEECH

The Spiritual Perspective

THE WHOLE is a drama of the most powerful kind. More than two thousand years have elapsed since the trial was enacted, but Plato's account of it still grips the reader with unspent force. Certain sentences, certain gestures of Socrates and certain episodes may be accurately reproduced in the text; but Plato's real concern is to render visible the forces which strove for the mastery and the decisions which were involved.

It is a strange defence that Socrates makes. Involuntarily one thinks of Euthyphro as present. One seems to see him moving invisibly through the speeches. Often it is as if Socrates—the Socrates of Plato, who is also of course that of the first dialogue—is himself thinking of him; for instance, when he says what line he would have to take in order to win his case before these judges. Beside this latent contrast the manner in which he pleads his case stands out clear and perilous.

If one looks more closely, one notices how the action shifts its perspective from the immediate circumstances to that which is humanly and spiritually more vital. In the actual foreground stands the accused, Socrates, son of Sophroniscus, a native of Alopece and a stonemason—or sculptor—by trade, who has to answer before the supreme court to charges of religious impiety and leading young men astray. But in fact he does something quite different. He presents himself before a spiritual court: before Apollo, to whom he is conscious of a special obligation, and gives him an account of how he has carried out the god's mission; he appears before his own conscience, and examines himself as to whether he has done what was right. Through these two transactions there runs yet another, a third. In this Socrates himself is the accuser and demands an account from his judges before the tribunal of Truth. And they too have seen this, for he has more than once "to admonish the gentlemen not to make an uproar and shout interruptions".

The Introduction

The prosecution has read its indictment and argued for it, and Socrates begins his defence:

I cannot tell what impression my accusers have made upon you, Athenians: for my own part, I know that they nearly made me forget who I was, so plausible were they; and yet they have scarcely uttered one single word of truth.

Cutting irony, which at once receives further emphasis:

But of all their many falsehoods, the one which astonished me most was when they said that I was a clever speaker, and that you must be careful not to let me mislead you. I thought that it was most impudent of them not to be ashamed to talk in that way;

> *for as soon as I open my mouth the lie will be exposed, and I shall prove that I am not a clever speaker in any way at all: unless, indeed, by a clever speaker they mean a man who speaks the truth. If that is their meaning, I agree with them that I am a much greater orator than they. My accusers, then I repeat, have said little or nothing that is true; but from me you shall hear the whole truth. Certainly you will not hear an elaborate speech, Athenians, drest up, like theirs, with words and phrases. I will say to you what I have to say, without preparation, and in the words which come first.*

And again:

> *The truth is this. I am more than seventy years old, and this is the first time that I have ever come before a Court of Law; so your manner of speech here is quite strange to me. If I had been really a stranger, you would have forgiven me for speaking in the language and the fashion of my native country: and so now I ask you to grant me what I think I have a right to claim. Never mind the style of my speech—it may be better or it may be worse—give your whole attention to the question, Is what I say just, or is it not? That is what makes a good judge, as speaking the truth makes a good advocate.*

This defines his standpoint and that of his judges too.

The accusers with whom he has to deal fall into two groups. On one side are the movers of the formal indictment; on the other, the many everywhere with their talk, who have always been against him and now find their sentiments expressed by Meletus. They too say

> *that there is one Socrates, a wise man, who speculates about the heavens, and who examines into all things that are beneath the earth, and who can "make the worse appear the better reason".*

These latter are the more dangerous, because there is no getting at them. They see in Socrates an innovator; a sophist, who confuses good and evil, true and false; a man without **reverence**, who breaks through what is secret, directs impious criticism at what is holy, and so imperils the foundations of human existence:

> *And the most unreasonable thing of all is that commonly I do not even know their names: I cannot tell you who they are, except in the case of the comic poets.*[1] *But all the rest who have been trying to prejudice you against me, from motives of spite and jealousy, and sometimes, it may be, from conviction, are the enemies whom it is hardest to meet. For I cannot call any one of them forward in Court, to cross-examine him: I have, as it were, simply to fight with shadows in my defence, and to put questions which there is no one to answer.*

Socrates has soon disposed of the tangible part of the accusation, which was as follows:

> "*Socrates is an evil-doer, who meddles with inquiries into things beneath the earth, and in heaven, and who 'makes the worse appear the better reason,' and who teaches others these same things.*"

To this he replies:

> *But, the truth is, Athenians, I have nothing to do with these matters, and almost all of you are yourselves my witnesses of this. I beg all of you who have ever heard me converse, and they are many, to inform your neighbours and tell them if any of you have ever heard me conversing about such matters, either more or less. That will show you that the other common stories about me are as false as this one.*

Nor has he the slightest ambition to be a teacher of youth and even to take money for this, as the Sophists do—large sums too, to judge from a conversation he has had with the wealthy Callias, who had to pay five minae to Evenus of Paros for the education of his sons:

> *Then I thought that Evenus was a fortunate person if he really understood this art and could teach so cleverly. If I had possessed*

---

[1] Like Aristophanes, who in his comedy *The Clouds* ridiculed the eccentric and disquieting philosopher.

knowledge of that kind, I should have given myself airs and prided myself on it. But, Athenians, the truth is that I do not possess it.

All this would be of no importance in itself; but it is a limited and inadequate expression for something deeper. So he now seeks to bring out this, the real point, and does it with such penetration that what began as a harmless matter rapidly takes on an air of ineluctability:

> *Perhaps some of you may reply: But, Socrates, what is this pursuit of yours? Whence come these calumnies against you? You must have been engaged in some pursuit out of the common. All these stories and reports of you would never have gone about, if you had not been in some way different from other men. So tell us what your pursuits are, that we may not give our verdict in the dark. I think that that is a fair question, and I will try to explain to you what it is that has raised these calumnies against me, and given me this name. Listen, then: some of you perhaps will think that I am jesting; but I assure you that I will tell you the whole truth. I have gained this name, Athenians, simply by reason of a certain wisdom. But by what kind of wisdom?*

Now he has to say something big; so he takes precautions against the indignation that he sees coming:

> *Do not interrupt me, Athenians, even if you think that I am speaking arrogantly. What I am going to say is not my own: I will tell you who says it, and he is worthy of your credit. I will bring the god of Delphi to be the witness of the fact of my wisdom and of its nature. You remember Chaerephon. From youth upwards he was my comrade; and he went into exile with the people, and with the people he returned. And you remember, too, Chaerephon's character; how vehement he was in carrying through whatever he took in hand. Once he went to Delphi and ventured to put this question to the oracle,—I entreat you again, my friends, not to cry out,—he asked, if there was any man who was wiser than I: and the priestess answered that there was no man. Chaerephon himself is dead, but his brother here will confirm what I say.*

As for himself, Socrates has not understood the oracle:

> *When I heard of the oracle I began to reflect: What can God mean by this dark saying? I know very well that I am not wise, even in the smallest degree. Then what can he mean by saying that I am the wisest of men? It cannot be that he is speaking falsely, for he is a god and cannot lie.*

Socrates cannot understand how he, who has so few illusions about himself, can be called the wisest of men, and that by a god who "cannot lie". Then he hits on a way out. One is not quite sure whether Plato's story is an apotheosis of his master's peculiar character, or a disguised irony aimed at the oracle—if one cannot make up one's mind to take it as simply true. Socrates, then, goes to the various people who have a reputation for wisdom, and talks to them,

> *thinking that there, if anywhere, I should prove the answer wrong, and meaning to point out to the oracle its mistake, and to say, "You said that I was the wisest of men, but this man is wiser than I am."*

And what is the result?

> *So I examined the man—I need not tell you his name, he was a politician—but this was the result, Athenians. When I conversed with him I came to see that, though a great many persons, and most of all he himself, thought that he was wise, yet he was not wise. And then I tried to prove to him that he was not wise, though he fancied that he was: and by so doing I made him, and many of the bystanders, my enemies. So when I went away, I thought to myself, "I am wiser than this man: neither of us probably knows anything that is really good, but he thinks that he has knowledge, when he has not, while I, having no knowledge, do not think that I have. I seem, at any rate, to be a little wiser than he is on this point: I do not think that I know what I do not know."*

As with this man, so is his subsequent experience with many others. Socrates goes the round, and wherever he sees that someone feels sure of himself, pretends to knowledge, or claims authority, he knocks at his door. He has to conclude that very little real, demonstrable insight exists—and strangely enough the less of it, the more brilliant the reputation for knowledge of the persons examined, while the less esteemed can show something more substantial. At the same time he notices with alarm that no one thanks him for his service to truth, but that on the contrary he is making himself disliked everywhere. Thus he tells in detail of this curious voyage of discovery to different kinds of men: politicians, poets, artisans—one notes the allusion to the three accusers—and it is a discouraging report. Socrates appears to be describing only the singular position in which the oracle has placed him, and most resolutely disclaims any personal competence. Yet the claim is there, arising in fact from the words of the Pythian priestess, which appear to be a divine approval of the Socratic way. In the last resort Socrates must raise this claim. He knows that he is indeed different from other men. He knows that something speaks out of him which finds utterance nowhere else. But if that is so, the contradiction which shows itself everywhere means that men, views and institutions, in a word the existing order of things, are refusing obedience to the divine behest.

The old men—most of them, we should say, for not a few of the older generation are attached to Socrates—most of the old men have turned a deaf ear to his message. So the young men come to him. The man "touched by the god, not merely a bearer of the thyrsus, but a true initiate", as it is said in the *Phaedo*, is understood by the young. They get great fun out of the examination conducted by Socrates, and take a hand in it themselves—and we need no very lively fancy to imagine how much clumsy handling there must have been here, how much precious heritage shattered and how much honourable susceptibility affronted; for in the rough and tumble of everyday life intellectual motives work out differently than in the purity of the idea or the atmosphere of an inspired circle. The rift between the generations widens. For those who feel themselves threatened in their very being Socrates is the corruptor. Their accusation has long been circulating in handy slogans: he holds forth on "heavenly phenomena and the things under the earth", that is, he arrogates to himself a knowledge about that which must remain hidden from man. He teaches people "to worship the gods in a way contrary to the common usage"—we remember the conversation with Euthyphro, which the latter, if he had been evilly disposed to Socrates, could have reported in a manner quite in the tenor of this accusation. He imparts to young people the pernicious "art of making the unjust cause appear just" and of disturbing hallowed convictions by irreverent criticism.

On these grounds Meletus and Anytus and Lycon have attacked me. Meletus is indignant with me on the part of the poets, and Anytus on the part of the artisans and politicians, and Lycon on the part of the orators.

He might, however, have added that there was yet another accuser: the rightful anxiety of all those who see danger to costly values of human, political and religious life, and cannot bring themselves to sacrifice these for the sake of a new will which has not yet proved itself.

The Accusation of the Three

Socrates now turns more specifically to the formal indictment:

He says that Socrates is an evildoer who corrupts the youth, and who does not believe in the gods whom the city believes in, but in other new divinities. Such is the charge. Let us examine each point in it separately.

But he answers in such a way as to continue the very activity with which the prosecution has charged him: he treats the speaker Meletus as one of the long line of those who pretend to know without really knowing, and carry out responsible undertakings without proving themselves fit for them by adequate insight and formation of character; and he applies to him the test imposed by the oracle.

Meletus says that I do wrong by corrupting the youth: but I say, Athenians, that he is doing wrong; for he is playing off a solemn jest by bringing men lightly to trial, and pretending to have a great zeal and interest in matters to which he has never given a moment's thought.

And now begins a real Socratic dialogue—very unconventional and yet in most deadly earnest, for the immediate issue, as in all those discussions in the gymnasium and in friends' houses and later in the market-place, is concerned with truth; but there is a further issue, for this once, of life and death.

> *Come here, Meletus. Is it not a fact that you think it very important that the younger men should be as excellent as possible?*
> MELETUS. *It is.*
> SOCRATES. *Come then: tell the judges, who is it who improves them? You take so much interest in the matter that of course you know that. You are accusing me, and bringing me to trial, because, as you say, you have discovered that I am the corrupter of the youth. Come now, reveal to the judges who improves them. You see, Meletus, you have nothing to say; you are silent. But don't you think that this is a scandalous thing? Is not your silence a conclusive proof of what I say, that you have never given a moment's thought to the matter?*

It must be a strange experience for Meletus. He is quite ready for an argument, but one which would turn on concrete cases, discuss alleged statements, seek to weaken the impression produced by the prosecution—in a word, he is prepared for the arts of advocate. Instead of which—such questions! So he remains silent; but Socrates does not loose his hold:

> *Come, tell us, my good sir, who makes the young men better citizens?*
> MEL. *The laws.*
> SOCR. *My excellent sir, that is not my question. What man improves the young, who starts with a knowledge of the laws?*

It is obvious that the laws, the norms of the community's life, regulate activity for good; the question is, which men, in practice and by their influence, act in the spirit of the laws. So Meletus answers more precisely—and like an opportunist too, with a bow to the powers of the moment, the jurors. But this very answer gives the adept of irony his cue:

MEL. *The judges here, Socrates.*

SOCR. *What do you mean, Meletus? Can they educate the young and improve them?*

MEL. *Certainly.*

SOCR. *All of them? or only some of them?*

MEL. *All of them.*

SOCR. *By Hêrê that is good news! There is a great abundance of benefactors. And do the listeners here improve them, or not?*

MEL. *They do.*

SOCR. *And do the senators?*

MEL. *Yes.*

SOCR. *Well then, Meletus; do the members of the Assembly corrupt the younger men? or do they again all improve them?*

MEL. *They too improve them.*

SOCR. *Then all the Athenians, apparently, make the young into fine fellows, except me, and I alone corrupt them. Is that your meaning?*

MEL. *Most certainly; that is my meaning.*

SOCR. *You have discovered me to be a most unfortunate man.*

And here another trait in Socrates's character comes out. From opposition, presumably, to all that is academic, pompous and high-flown, he keeps referring us, even in the most serious questions, to the simplest facts of everyday life:

> *Now tell me: do you think that the same holds good in the case of horses? Does one man do them harm and every one else improve them? On the contrary, is it not one man only, or a very few—namely, those who are skilled in horses—who can improve them; while the majority of men harm them, if they use them, and have to do with them?*

High quality is always the privilege of the few. That which is common to all cannot rank high in the scale. But if the improvement of youth is really an art so universally practised, it will hardly be Socrates who lacks it. Rather he will probably be one of those very few who understand the art of forming men by truth and love. But if—the next section points out—he really does harm to the young, that can only be from ignorance. For no one will knowingly do something which is harmful to the general wellbeing, since such harm invariably recoils on its author—a form of argument, one must admit, which presupposes an advanced maturity of mind. The multitude will hardly feel it to be a proof, and in Socrates's case it was not in fact felt to be such:

> *And if I corrupt them unintentionally, the law does not call upon you to prosecute me for a fault like that, which is an involuntary one; you should take me aside and adomonish and instruct me; for of course I shall cease from doing wrong involuntarily, as soon as I know that I have been doing wrong.*

The last sentence expresses a great integrity of moral disposition, which seeks what is right under all circumstances, and to which therefore, the moment an action is recognized as wrong, the motive for doing it ceases. It also shows the principle from which a pregnant thesis would be evolved in Plato's future works: that the essence of virtue lies in knowledge. This thesis asserts more than the general significance which knowledge has for moral action, particularly when it is a question of a cognitive experience so important as that of Socratic and Platonic theory. "Knowledge" here means rather the special knowledge which consists in the contemplation of the Idea. To contemplate the Idea means to enter into the region and condition of mental receptivity; not merely to see what is true and to see it truly, but also—at the actual moment and in the actual cognitive relation—to take on the mould of truth oneself. But as the Idea, as will be shown more explicitly, is rooted in the ultimate "Being" as such, that is, in the Good, reference to it brings the Good into the sphere of existence.

Resuming the argument, Socrates now comes to the point by which the Athenians, concerned for their piety, were most affected.

> *However, now tell us, Meletus, how do you say that I corrupt the younger men? Clearly, according to your indictment, by teaching them not to believe in the gods of the city, but in other new divinities instead. You mean that I corrupt young men by that teaching, do you not?*

MEL. *Yes: most certainly; I mean that.*

SOCR. *Then in the name of these gods of whom we are speaking, explain yourself a little more clearly to me and to the judges here. I cannot understand what you mean. Do you mean that I teach young men to believe in some gods, but not in the gods of the city? Do you accuse me of teaching them to believe in strange gods? If that is your meaning, I myself believe in some gods, and my crime is not that of absolute atheism. Or do you mean that I do not believe in the gods at all myself, and that I teach other people not to believe in them either?*

MEL. *I mean that you do not believe in the gods in any way whatever.*

SOCR. *Wonderful Meletus! Why do you say that? Do you mean that I believe neither the sun nor the moon to be gods, like other men?*

Meletus thinks he can hook his opponent here:

I swear he does not, judges: he says that the sun is a stone, and the moon earth.

But he has little success with this point, for so much is already a commonplace among the educated: that the heavenly bodies are not as such, physically so to speak, deities.

SOCR. *My dear Meletus, do you think that you are prosecuting Anaxagoras? You must have a poor opinion of the judges, and think them very unlettered men, if you imagine that they do not know that the works of Anaxagoras of Clazomenae are full of these doctrines. And so young men learn these things from me, when they can often buy places in the theatre for a drachma at most, and laugh Socrates to scorn, were he to pretend that these doctrines, which are very peculiar doctrines too, were his.*

So not to believe in the divinity of the solar body is not godlessness —especially when at the same time one insists so earnestly that one is in the service of Apollo, as Socrates does. What, then, is the prosecution aiming at?

But please tell me, do you really think that I do not believe in the gods at all?

MEL. *Most certainly I do. You are a complete atheist.*

SOCR. *No one believes that, Meletus, and I think that you know it to be a lie yourself. It seems to me, Athenians, that Meletus is a very insolent and wanton man, and that he is prosecuting me simply in the insolence and wantonness of youth. He is like a man trying an experiment on me, by asking me a riddle that has no answer. "Will this wise Socrates," he says to himself, "see that I am jesting and contradicting myself? or shall I outwit him and every one else who hears me?" Meletus seems to me to contradict himself in his indictment: it is as if he were to say, "Socrates is a wicked man who does not believe in the gods, but who believes in the gods." But that is mere trifling.*

Now, my friends, let us see why I think that this is his meaning. Do you answer me, Meletus: and do you, Athenians, remember the request which I made to you at starting, and do not interrupt me if I talk in my usual way.

Is there any man, Meletus, who believes in the existence of things pertaining to men and not in the existence of men? Make him answer the question, my friends, without these absurd interruptions. Is there any man who believes in the existence of horsemanship and not in the existence of horses? or in flute-playing and not in flute-players? There is not, my excellent sir. If you will not answer, I will tell both you and the judges that. But you must answer my next question. Is there any man who believes in the existence of divine things and not in the existence of divinities?[1]

MEL. *There is not.*

SOCR. *I am very glad that the judges have managed to extract an answer from you. Well then, you say that I believe in divine beings, whether they be old or new ones, and that I teach others to believe in them; at any rate, according to your statement, I believe in divine beings. That you have sworn in your deposition. But if I believe in divine beings, I suppose it follows necessarily that I believe in divinities. Is it not so? It is. I assume that you grant that, as you do not answer. But do we not believe that divinities are*

---

[1] The word *daimones* has not the meaning it conveys in our usage, but means divine beings of inferior rank; see the passage immediately following.

APOLOGY 43

either gods themselves or the children of the gods? Do you admit that?
MEL. *I do.*
SOCR. *Then you admit that I believe in divinities: now, if these divinities are gods, then, as I say, you are jesting and asking a riddle, and asserting that I do not believe in the gods, and at the same time that I do, since I believe in divinities. But if these divinities are the illegitimate children of the gods, either by the nymphs or by other mothers, as they are said to be, then, I ask, what man could believe in the existence of the children of the gods, and not in the existence of the gods? That would be as strange as believing in the existence of the offspring of horses and asses, and not in the existence of horses and asses.*

It is hardly to be assumed that Socrates believed seriously in "illegitimate children of the gods, either by the nymphs or by other mothers"; at any rate he did not regard the *Daimonion*, of which he was so often heard to speak, as such a hybrid creature. It is evident from the whole manner in which he refers to it in the course of the first and third speeches, that he experienced it as a power intimately related to the core of his own existence and of a very pure numinous character. His argument, then, is to be understood as entirely *ad hominem*, directed at the man he is talking to. He wants to make the following point clear to Meletus: "You say that I believe in daemons, though you imagine by them beings which are incompatible with the dignity of real gods. That is absurd; but even in your absurd thoughts there is the law of cause and effect. Therefore you must not assert that I deny the gods, when—in accordance with your use of the word daemon—I believe in their bastards."

The proof is in itself valid, but it does not answer the real question raised by Meletus and those who share his views. They are concerned, not about the question whether Socrates believes in spiritually active divine powers and, behind these, in a sublimely conceived Divinity, but whether he believes in the ancient gods of the state, and that in the direct and concrete sense supposed by the traditional religious mentality. That, however, they perceive accurately, is not the case. When Socrates talks of Apollo, it is something different from the Apollo meant by anyone else, anyone who lives by tradition; and the mythically minded Athenians can make nothing of the *Daimonion* of whose protection Socrates is conscious. It is their Apollo and their *Daimonion* that they are concerned about, for with these the whole existing order of things hangs together. And as they do not recognize the new values which are emerging in Socrates's conception of religion, they feel him to be a danger to religion in general, and express this danger in the sort of ideas which they have at their command.

Socrates's fate is tragic. The true nature of tragedy, however, lies in the fact that good is ruined, not by what is evil and senseless, but by another good which also has its rights; and that this hostile good is too narrow and selfish to see the superior right or the destined hour of the other, but has power enough to trample down the other's claim. The events of the dialogues we are engaged on would be robbed of their peculiar seriousness if we were to see in Socrates only the great and innocent man misunderstood, and in his accusers only the narrow-minded mob clinging to what is old. The truth, which must be emphasized again and again, is that here an epoch—a declining one, it is true, but one still full of values—confronts a man who, great as he is and called to be a bringer of new things, disrupts by his spirit all that has hitherto held sway. In the incompatibility of these two opposing sets of values and forces lies the real tragedy of the situation.

Socrates now resumes the story of the oracle:

> *But, I repeat, it is certainly true, as I have already told you, that I have incurred much unpopularity and made many enemies. And that is what will cause my condemnation, if I am condemned; not Meletus, nor Anytus either, but the prejudice and suspicion of the multitude. They have been the destruction of many good men before me, and I think that they will be so again. There is no fear that I shall be their last victim.*

But he now hears a reproach from another side, that of practical commonsense, which sees foolishness in his whole manner of acting.

Perhaps some one will say: "Are you not ashamed, Socrates, of following pursuits which are very likely now to cause your death?"

Here comes to light the inmost pathos of the man bound by duty to the spirit:

I should answer him with justice, and say: "My friend, if you think that a man of any worth at all ought to reckon the chances of life and death when he acts, or that he ought to think of anything but whether he is acting rightly or wrongly, and as a good or a bad man would act, you are grievously mistaken."

For this obligation he appeals to the warriors before Troy, Achilles especially; and then follow the grand words:

For this, Athenians, I believe to be the truth. Wherever a man's post is, whether he has chosen it of his own will, or whether he has been placed at it by his commander, there it is his duty to remain and face the danger, without thinking of death, or of any other thing, except dishonour.

From height to height the mind of this heroic philosopher unfolds itself—one who is well called heroic in the deepest sense, though he himself would probably have repudiated this designation with scorn:

When the generals whom you choose to command me, Athenians, placed me at my post at Potidaea, and at Amphipolis, and at Delium, I remained where they placed me, and ran the risk of death, like other men: and it would be very strange conduct on my part if I were to desert my post now from fear of death or of any other thing, when God has commanded me, as I am persuaded that he has done, to spend my life in searching for wisdom, and in examining myself and others.

This is not merely a simple sense of duty—in itself grand enough —but the purest spiritual and religious consciousness of a mission. And the courage which inspires the words is in close relation with the experience of truth:

> *That would indeed be a very strange thing: and then certainly I might with justice be brought to trial for not believing in the gods: for I should be disobeying the oracle, and fearing death, and thinking myself wise, when I was not wise. For to fear death, my friends, is only to think ourselves wise, without being wise: for it is to think that we know what we do not know.*

And not only philosophy, but wisdom and a wonderful maturity of soul are heard in the next sentences:

> *For anything that men can tell, death may be the greatest good that can happen to them: but they fear it as if they knew quite well that it was the greatest of evils. And what is this but that shameful ignorance of thinking that we know what we do not know? In this matter too, my friends, perhaps I am different from the mass of mankind: and if I were to claim to be at all wiser than others, it would be because I do not think that I have any clear knowledge about the other world, when, in fact, I have none. But I do know very well that it is evil and base to do wrong, and to disobey my superior, whether he be man or god.*

The pathos mounts. What he has done does not need to be defended against accusation, but he is right in upholding it to the utmost.

> *And so, even if you acquit me now, and do not listen to Anytus' argument that, if I am to be acquitted, I ought never to have been brought to trial at all; and that, as it is, you are bound to put me to death, because, as he said, if I escape, all your children will forthwith be utterly corrupted by practising what Socrates teaches; if you were therefore to say to me, "Socrates, this time we will not listen to Anytus: we will let you go; but on this condition, that you cease from carrying on this search of yours, and from philosophy; if you are found following those pursuits again, you shall die": I say, if you offered to let me go on these terms, I should reply:—"Athenians, I hold you in the highest regard and love; but I will obey God rather than you: and as long as I have breath and strength I will not cease from philosophy, and from exhorting you, and declaring the truth to*

every one of you whom I meet, saying, as I am wont, 'My excellent friend, you are a citizen of Athens, a city which is very great and very famous for wisdom and power of mind; are you not ashamed of caring so much for the making of money, and for reputation, and for honour? Will you not think or care about wisdom, and truth, and the perfection of your soul?' And if he disputes my words, and says that he does care about these things, I shall not forthwith release him and go away: I shall question him and cross-examine him and test him: and if I think that he has not virtue, though he says that he has, I shall reproach him for setting the lower value on the most important things, and a higher value on those that are of less account."

The emotion becomes still more powerful:

For, know well, God has commanded me to do so. And I think that no better piece of fortune has ever befallen you in Athens than my service to God. For I spend my whole life in going about and persuading you all to give your first and chiefest care to the perfection of your souls, and not till you have done that to think of your bodies, or your wealth; and telling you that virtue does not come from wealth, but that wealth, and every other good thing which men have, whether in public, or in private, comes from virtue. If then I corrupt the youth by this teaching, the mischief is great: but if any man says that I teach anything else, he speaks falsely. And therefore, Athenians, I say, either listen to Anytus, or do not listen to him: either acquit me, or do not acquit me: but be sure that I shall not alter my way of life; no, not if I have to die for it many times.

Once more the marvellous pathos of this speech rises higher—though it is so far from pathetic in the ordinary sense, since it comes straight from reality:

Be sure that if you put me to death, who am what I have told you that I am, you will do yourselves more harm than me. Meletus and Anytus can do me no harm: that is impossible: for I am sure that God will not allow a good man to be injured by a bad one. They may indeed kill me, or drive me into exile, or deprive me of my civil rights; and perhaps Meletus and others think those things great evils. But I do not think so: I think that it is a much greater evil to do what he is doing now, and to try to put a man to death unjustly.

And then a very earnest warning:

And now, Athenians, I am not arguing in my own defence at all, as you might expect me to do: I am trying to persuade you not to sin against God, by condemning me, and rejecting his gift to you. For if you put me to death, you will not easily find another man to fill my place. God has sent me to attack the city, as if it were a great and noble horse, to use a quaint simile, which was rather sluggish from its size, and which needed to be aroused by a gadfly: and I think that I am the gadfly that God has sent to the city to attack it; for I never cease from settling upon you, as it were, at every point, and rousing, and exhorting, and reproaching each man of you all day long. You will not easily find any one else, my friends, to fill my place: and if you take my advice, you will spare my life. You are vexed, as drowsy persons are, when they are awakened, and of course, if you listened to Anytus, you could easily kill me with a single blow, and then sleep on undisturbed for the rest of your lives, unless God were to care for you enough to send another man to arouse you.

Before such a conviction the accusations of impiety lose all their substance. Yet one feels that this conviction is not understood, indeed that its very sincerity causes it to be felt by the accusers as a fresh proof for their point of view. For it is just the unprecedented human, spiritual and religious force of this conviction that makes it a danger to the established order.

So even the proof that Socrates adduces for the purity of his motives—namely, that he has renounced riches and power for the sake of his service—will make no difference to the state of his case; on the contrary, it will only underline the dangerousness of the man:

And you may easily see that it is God who has given me to your city: a mere human impulse would never have led me to neglect all my own interests, or to endure seeing my private affairs neglected now for so many years, while it made me busy myself unceasingly in your interests, and go to each man of you by himself, like a father, or an elder brother, trying to persuade him to care for virtue. There

> would have been a reason for it, if I had gained any advantage by this conduct, or if I had been paid for my exhortations; but you see yourselves that my accusers, though they accuse me of everything else without blushing, have not had the effrontery to say that I ever either exacted or demanded payment. They could bring no evidence of that. And I think that I have sufficient evidence of the truth of what I say in my poverty.

For the same reason he has also held aloof from public affairs:

> Perhaps it may seem strange to you that, though I am so busy in going about in private with my counsel, yet I do not venture to come forward in the assembly, and take part in the public councils. You have often heard me speak of my reason for this, and in many places: it is that I have a certain divine sign from God, which is the divinity that Meletus has caricatured in his indictment.

This passage is important, because Socrates here explicitly professes his faith in the mysterious voice:

> I have had it from childhood: it is a kind of voice, which whenever I hear it, always turns me back from something which I was going to do, but never urges me to act.

The description indicates that in this "kind of divine and daemonic voice" we are not dealing with reason; for this the call has too much of the objectively encountered as well as of the mysterious. We might think rather of the admonition of conscience; but the "voice" cannot be identified with this either, since it never does more than say what must not be done, while the admonition of conscience can convey a "thou shalt" as well as a "thou shalt not". It is a question rather of a primarily religious experience. This becomes quite clear when we take into consideration what Socrates, now condemned to death, says in his third speech to those of the judges who had voted for his acquittal (40a—b). He tells them how the interior warning has opposed itself "even on the most trivial occasions," when he was "about to do something in the wrong way". That, of course, could equally well be the prohibition of conscience expressing itself; but what follows, according to which it has often stopped him in the middle of what he was saying, shows that the "voice" has the character of something instantaneous and coming from elsewhere, which places it rather in the vicinity of prophecy. The result is the same when he calls it "the familiar soothsaying, that of the *Daimonion*", "the sign of the god"—appellations which obviously belong to the sphere of religion, or more specifically that of prophecy.

The figure of Socrates has a many-sidedness which is at first sight confusing. He is ugly, and yet Alcibiades in his *Symposium* speech associates the golden images of the gods with him; he has a relentlessly penetrating intellect and is yet ruled by Eros; he is full of criticism and irony, always ready to oppose a questionable emotion with the most workaday reality, and yet led by a mysterious guidance. That this guidance never commands, but only forbids, increases the credibility of the account. A certain arbitrariness attaches to it on this score, which harmonizes with the irrationality of the religious element as well as with the man's personality. It would certainly be far-fetched to call Socrates a seer; his centre of gravity lies too much in the philosophical. But when we consider, on the one hand, how reverent his nature is, and on the other hand, how relentlessly he puts people into a position of new and dangerous responsibility, we have to ask ourselves whence he gets the authority and power to do this. Socrates is no absolutist; rather he is suspicious of any over-positive assertion, sceptical towards himself, and deeply conscious of his responsibility towards men, over whom he has such power. What makes him, as a living and feeling man, equal to his own task? His attitude has something ambiguous about it. He shakes the stability of old institutions, but puts no new construction in their place, only a seeking, enquiring, doubting. He is one of those men who exercise an inexplicable influence without actually being leaders or proposing definite aims. What keeps him in this suspense and enables him to produce the effect he does from it? In the last resort the only possible answer seems to be that it is something religious. Even if he did not really make the three speeches of the *Apology* before the court, at any rate they represent the justification of his master's activity given by Plato. Even if the oracle story should not be taken as simple fact, it would still express some ultimate reality which the great disciple perceived behind the figure of his master. The existence and activity of Socrates are rooted in the consciousness of a divine mission. This is expressed in a certain belief or trust, but stands also in relation with an original religious experience which accompanies his whole activity, namely the "familiar soothsaying of the *Daimonion*."

> *It is this which forbids me to take part in politics. And I think that it does well to forbid me.*

In order to be able to speak of spiritual and divine things with complete freedom—in such a way that the words come from the heart of the subject and pierce to the vital centre of the hearer—the speaker must have separated himself from the ties of money and the struggle for power. The doctrine that the true philosopher's freedom is to be won by renunciation, a doctrine to be so powerfully developed in the *Phaedo*, is announced here.

> *And do not be vexed with me for telling the truth. There is no man who will preserve his life for long, either in Athens or elsewhere, if he firmly opposes the wishes of the people, and tries to prevent the commission of much injustice and illegality in the State. He who would really fight for justice, must do so as a private man, not in public, if he means to preserve his life, even for a short time.*

As a proof that such abstention did not spring from cowardice, but simply from the nature of his task, Socrates recalls his conduct in times of crisis:

> *Listen then to what has happened to me, that you may know that there is no man who could make me consent to do wrong from the fear of death; but that I would perish at once rather than give way. What I am going to tell you may be a commonplace in the Courts of Law; nevertheless it is true. The only office that I ever held in the State, Athenians, was that of Senator. When you wished to try the ten generals, who did not rescue their men after the battle of Arginusae, in a body, which was illegal, as you all came to think afterwards, the tribe Antiochis, to which I belong, held the presidency. On that*

occasion I alone of all the presidents opposed your illegal action, and gave my vote against your illegal action, and gave my vote against you. The speakers were ready to suspend me and arrest me; and you were clamouring against me, and crying out to me to submit. But I thought that I ought to face the danger out in the cause of law and justice, rather than join with you in your unjust proposal, from fear of imprisonment or death. That was before the destruction of the democracy. When the oligarchy came, the Thirty sent for me, with four others, to the Council-Chamber, and ordered us to bring over Leon the Salaminian from Salamis, that they might put him to death. They were in the habit of frequently giving similar orders to many others, wishing to implicate as many men as possible in their crimes.

So he can say:

But then again I proved, not by mere words, but by my actions, that, if I may use a vulgar expression, I do not care a straw for death; but that I do care very much indeed about not doing anything against the laws of God or man.

Another key-phrase is heard in this passage: "I have never been any man's teacher." The nature of his intellectual activity is connected with the nature and ethos of his knowledge. The man who is always reiterating that he knows nothing cannot exercise any activity based on the supposition that he has certain and communicable items of knowledge at his command. He can but give what he has: the knowledge of what true insight must be; the acknowledgment that one does not yet possess it; the will to attain it at any cost. He can arouse the conscience with regard to truth and bring the desire for truth to the region of actuality. That, however, is something quite different from the idea of teaching made current by the Sophists.

I have never withheld myself from any one, young or old, who was anxious to hear me converse while I was about my mission; neither do I converse for payment, and refuse to converse without payment: I am ready to ask questions of rich and poor alike, and if any man wishes to answer me, and then listen to what I have to say, he may.

And I cannot justly be charged with causing these men to turn out good or bad citizens: for I never either taught, or professed to teach any of them any knowledge whatever.

But, it might be objected here, whence then comes his power of attracting the young? Must there not be some other appeal—something exciting, seductive, destructive? To this Socrates gives the answer: I am an old man. I have been at work among you for a long time. Many who listened to me as young men have now reached mature years, and have had time to test by experience what they learnt with me. Ask them!

And he mentions a number of such, who listened to his discourses and are now present in this assembly. The author of the *Apology* indirectly secures for himself a place among these by including in their number "Adimantus, son of Aristo and brother of Plato here" (33d—34a).

Socrates is perfectly aware how much his method of defence is opposed to all usual procedure:

There may be some one among you who will be vexed when he remembers how, even in a less important trial than this, he prayed and entreated the judges to acquit him with many tears, and brought forward his children and many of his friends and relatives in Court, in order to appeal to your feelings; and then finds that I shall do none of these things, though I am in what he would think the supreme danger. Perhaps he will harden himself against me when he notices this: it may make him angry, and he may give his vote in anger.

The danger is great but he can make no concession.

It is not from arrogance, Athenians, nor because I hold you cheap: whether or no I can face death bravely is another question: but for my own credit, and for your credit, and for the credit of our city, I do not think it well, at my age, and with my name, to do anything of that kind. Rightly or wrongly, men have made up their minds that in some way Socrates is different from the mass of mankind.

Not only his self-respect forbids him to plead his cause in such a way, but also—and again the thought takes the philosophical step into the essential—the idea of the just and of justice itself:

> *He (the judge) does not sit to give away justice to his friends, but to pronounce judgment: and he has sworn not to favour any man whom he would like to favour, but to decide questions according to law.*

True piety is to see that right and law are rooted in the divine, and to act accordingly:

> *For were I to be successful, and to prevail on you by my prayers to break your oaths, I should be clearly teaching you to believe that there are no gods; and I should be simply accusing myself by my defence of not believing in them. But, Athenians, that is very far from the truth. I do believe in the gods as no one of my accusers believes in them: and to you and to God I commit my cause to be decided as is best for you and for me.*

The question as to the essence of piety remained without a proper answer in the *Euthyphro*. Socrates could not elicit the answer from his interlocutor, and did not give it himself. Nevertheless some elements of the idea emerged in the course of the dialogue and are more fully worked out in the *Apology*. These—like the definitions of Plato's early works in general—have a special value because the impress of Socrates's personality is particularly vivid in them.

According to these indications piety means above all things an effort to apprehend the divine. It means not sticking fast in traditional ideas, but enquiring after the essence, and thinking this essence as purely and worthily as the best powers of the mind are able. In this process contradictions of tradition and environment may appear; the divine may raise itself to heights far above the familiar, natural ideas, and thus there may occur a kind of religious emptying-out of immediate existence. But all this must then be endured for truth's sake, for the truth of the divine itself.

If the divine soars so high that—to use the expression of the *Euthyphro*—it can no longer be brought into any kind of "commercial transaction", it is still not without its effect and demand on ordinary life. On the contrary, man must understand his life's truest task as a manifestation of the divine will. Socrates's statement that he deduced from the oracle at Delphi his mission to test men, is represented primarily as a biographical fact. But as such it contains the more profound claim that what he does is done in the service of Apollo, who is the god of brightness and creative inspiration. To do this is piety: obedience to the divine command in the activity of one's life. And this piety is put to the proof as soon as the divine commission comes into conflict with the demands of one's environment and has to be carried out with loss and danger. The relation of obedience comes out in an even more concrete form where Socrates alludes to the voice of the *Daimonion*. It speaks suddenly, without being prepared for by personal intuitions on the part of the one addressed; and piety means obeying it, even when its admonition is not perceived to be right, or when it speaks so suddenly that a sentence must be broken off in the middle. This experience too is primarily a biographical peculiarity of Socrates; behind it however, as something deeper and more universal, is that watchfulness for the numinous command which is evinced not by rational considerations, but only by its specifically religious validity.

A further element in the definition of piety will appear in the *Crito*, and may be anticipated here for the sake of the context. Socrates there tells his friend, who is trying to induce him to escape from prison, that it is not lawful to do so. Once the court's verdict has been formally given, it is binding on the condemned, and this obligation persists through all human contingencies. In the progress of the conversation the moral claim is given a figurative expression: the laws of the state appear as the powers who order and protect it, and they present their claims to Socrates. The nature of these claims surpasses the merely ethical and assumes a religious, nay ultimately a sheer dionysiac character. Piety, then, means understanding the validity of the morally good as something divine, and living up to it even at the cost of any temporal loss. From here there is a line of connection to the profound discussions of the *Phaedo*, in which the idea of the true is similarly treated. Truth is there experienced in such a manner that it appears as a self-revelation of the divine. To seek this truth without regard to anything else but its own validity, and thereby to be inwardly at one with the divinity which shines through the truth, is piety. This view subsequently finds its ultimate expression in the *Republic*, where behind the objective forms of truth, namely the Ideas, the mystery of the Good is discerned and associated with the image of the Sun.

THE SECOND SPEECH

The Introduction

THE JUDGES have now to decide on guilt or innocence in the sense of the accusation, and their verdict goes against Socrates. It is only by a narrow majority; of the five hundred members of the court only two hundred and eighty have pronounced "guilty". Thirty votes more in his favour would have given an even verdict, and Socrates would have been acquitted.

For many offences the penalty was provided by the law, for others it had to be fixed by the judges. In this case the condemned man had the option either of agreeing to the penalty proposed by the prosecution, or of himself making an alternative proposal. It was then for the court to decide between the two proposals. Socrates has therefore another chance of pleading his case and averting the death penalty. But once again his speech takes quite a different line from what prudence would have counselled:

> *I am not vexed at the verdict which you have given, Athenians, for many reasons. I expected that you would find me guilty; and I am not so much surprised at that, as at the numbers of the votes. I, certainly, never thought that the majority against me would have been so narrow. But now it seems that if only thirty votes had changed sides, I should have escaped.*

This has a curious sound—as though the speaker, with his experience of life, were surprised that so much perception should have been found among the number of his judges; or again, as though the philosopher were struck by the reflection on what trifles fate hangs.

The Alternative Proposal

He now brings forward his own proposal:

So he proposes death as the penalty. Be it so. And what counter-penalty shall I propose to you, Athenians? What I deserve, of course, must I not?

The phrase "what I deserve" is ambiguous. Prudence would have suggested saying: "If I am guilty, then no greater penalty than is really adequate to my guilt." That would have afforded an opportunity to disarm the judges' vengeance by a show of moderation. But Socrates puts the statement in a form of renewed aggressiveness: "I shall propose that I be given what I have a right to." The thought gathers itself up in a great effort:

What then do I deserve to pay or to suffer for having determined not to spend my life in ease? I neglected the things which most men value, such as wealth, and family interests, and military commands, and popular oratory, and all the political appointments, and clubs, and factions, that there are in Athens; for I thought that I was really too conscientious a man to preserve my life if I engaged in these matters. So I did not go where I should have done no good either to you or to myself. I went instead to each one of you by himself, to do him, as I say, the greatest of services, and strove to persuade him not to think of his affairs, until he had thought of himself, and tried to make himself as perfect and wise as possible; not to think of the affairs of Athens until he had thought of Athens herself; and in all cases to bestow his thoughts on things in the same manner. Then what do I deserve for such a life? Something good, Athenians, if I am really to propose what I deserve.

Then a fresh onset:

and something good which it would be suitable to me to receive. Then what is a suitable reward to be given to a poor benefactor, who requires leisure to exhort you? There is no reward, Athenians, so suitable for him as a public maintenance in the Prytaneum. It is a much more suitable reward for him than for any of you who has won a victory at the Olympic games with his horse or his chariots. Such a man only makes you seem happy, but I make you really happy: and he is not in want, and I am. So if I am to propose the penalty which I really deserve, I propose this, a public maintenance in the Prytaneum.

The Prytaneum was a public building in which the executive committee of the supreme council of state, honoured guests of the city, specially distinguished citizens and the victors in the Olympic games took their meals at the expense of the state. What a claim then! And the reason given for it contains in addition a side-thrust at the people's favourites, the Olympian victors.

The hearers are doubtless beside themselves—perhaps also they are mute with astonishment, for Socrates does not have to repeat his admonition not to "make an uproar". The reader, however, is conscious of a misgiving. Not that Socrates should plead "not guilty"; he has a perfect right to do so. Yet in a tragic sense he is "guilty"—guilty of the downfall of all the great and beautiful things which can no longer exist if the mentality which he stands for prevails. In history, however, one value must always give way for another to emerge, and only those who are happily—or wantonly—prejudiced believe in absolute progress. But Socrates is one of the happily prejudiced, like everyone who is engaged body and soul in a genuine mission. Nor is our misgiving concerned with his belief that he is a benefactor of the state and deserves, instead of punishment, the highest recognition. He is convinced of his task and has staked everything on it, therefore he may advance the claim. And the somewhat violent logic with which he maintains this claim is the peculiar style of the heroic philosopher, even though impaired by a little pedantry—and perhaps also by a little presumption, which lies however not so much in the man's personal will as in the fact that "philosophy" becomes the type of existence. For this is a highly problematical point, and much could be said about it, in spite of Plato and Nietzsche. No, the real misgiving lies in the manner in which Socrates challenges the judges—especially when one reflects that he is speaking, not as a young and impetuous swayer of minds, but as an old man and a teacher of the strictest conscientiousness.

The court is not a department of officials, but represents the general public of Athens, and the indictment expresses, not merely the malice of a few evil-wishers, but the concern of the people as attached to what is old and established. Socrates however does not behave as an accused man in presence of the highest authority of the law; he drops this character—in his bearing constantly, at critical moments even expressly—and becomes a teacher, admonisher, nay even a judge. Even that could be accounted for by the consciousness of his mission—quite apart from the fact that the office of judge was an essential part of full citizen rights, so that each citizen was potentially a judge and therefore had to watch over the laws. But Socrates does more, he provokes the court. The demand to be fed in the Prytaneum would necessarily produce the effect either of mockery or of such an underlining of all that the indictment attacked, that those members of the court who are not wholly on his side could hardly reply otherwise than with the severest verdict. And it would be a false affectation to say that Socrates could not speak otherwise. He could very well, and without compromising himself in the least. And the case would then go differently, for the first verdict has shown that a large proportion of the judges are in his favour. So the death-sentence can be averted, if the defendant keeps within bounds and spares the susceptibilities of his hearers. But there seems to be something in Socrates that makes for the extreme realization of his own pattern of mind, an impulse to set the seal of deed and destiny on the standpoint advanced in theory. He has been in opposition to the established order. This opposition has indeed brought him suspicion, enmity and ridicule; but he has been richly compensated by the adhesion and affection of so many of the best minds. But there seems to be in Socrates a conviction that a mission such as his ought not to be fulfilled peacefully, but must work itself out through ruin. That is why he provokes his own death. The motives at work here cannot be rationally accounted for. They are even assailable from a purely moral point of view. The sentence that Socrates provokes is according to his own conviction a crime, and will bring evil consequences on people and state. How can he act so—he who claims to speak with the deepest moral earnestness and to be wholly answerable to the truth ? Motives of a religious nature seem to be at work here: a consciousness that irruptions which touch the ultimate determination of existence must be paid for, not merely with labour or conflict, but with death.

The sentences which follow show in fact that Socrates knows well that he has said something monstrous:

> *Perhaps you think me stubborn and arrogant in what I am saying now, as in what I said about the entreaties and tears.*

He would be able to make his thoughts clear to them if he were allowed to conduct the dialogue of the case at greater length:

> *It is not so, Athenians; it is rather that I am convinced that I never wronged any man intentionally, though I cannot persuade you of that, for we have conversed together only a little time. If there were a law at Athens, as there is elsewhere, not to finish a trial of life and death in a single day, I think that I could have convinced you of it: but now it is not easy in so short a time to clear myself of the gross calumnies of my enemies.*

He must therefore let the appearance of presumption remain.

Then once more there emerges a wonderful philosophical and religious superiority:

> *Why should I? Lest I should suffer the penalty which Meletus proposes, when I say that I do not know whether it is a good or an evil? Shall I choose instead of it something which I know to be an evil, and propose that as a penalty?*

Whether death is an evil thing remains an open question; perhaps it is even a very good thing. But whatever might come into consideration as a milder penalty, would certainly be formidable:

> *Shall I propose imprisonment? And why should I pass the rest of my days in prison, the slave of successive officials? Or shall I propose a fine, with imprisonment until it is paid? I have told why I will not do that. I should have to remain in prison for I have no money to pay a fine with. Shall I then propose exile? Perhaps you would agree to that. Life would indeed be very dear to me, if I were unreasonable enough to expect that strangers would cheerfully*

tolerate my discussions and reasonings, when you who are my fellow-citizens cannot endure them, and have found them so burdensome and odious to you, that you are seeking now to be released from them. No, indeed, Athenians, that is not likely. A fine life I should lead for an old man, if I were to withdraw from Athens, and pass the rest of my days in wandering from city to city, and continually being expelled. For I know very well that the young men will listen to me, wherever I go, as they do here; and if I drive them away, they will persuade their elders to expel me: and if I do not drive them away, their fathers and kinsmen will expel me for their sakes.

But since an alternative proposal must be made, he makes it; and it sounds like a concession that a grown-up makes to children although there is no sense in it:

Perhaps I could pay you a mina: so I propose that. Plato here, Athenians, and Crito, and Critobulus, and Apollodorus bid me propose thirty minae, and they will be sureties for me. So I propose thirty minae. They will be sufficient sureties to you for the money.

After such a speech the outcome can scarcely be any longer in doubt. Plato's mention of his own name at this point sounds like an assurance that the *Apology* is a true report.

THE THIRD SPEECH

THE REPLY TO THE SENTENCE

AGAIN the judges confer, and the sentence ratifies the penalty proposed by the prosecution: death by the cup of hemlock.

The condemned man has now once more the opportunity to speak. He replies first to the sentence itself:

You have not gained very much time, Athenians, and, as the price of it, you will have an evil name from all who wish to revile the city, and they will cast in your teeth that you put Socrates, a wise man, to death. For they will certainly call me wise, whether I am wise or not, when they want to reproach you. If you would have waited for a little while, your wishes would have been fulfilled in the course of nature; for you see that I am an old man, far advanced in years, and near to death. I am speaking not to all of you, only to those who have voted for my death.

And again:

I have been defeated because I was wanting, not in arguments, but in overboldness and effrontery: because I would not plead before you as you would have liked to hear me plead, or appeal to you with weeping and wailing, or say and do many other things, which I maintain are unworthy of me, but which you have been accustomed to from other men. But when I was defending myself, I thought that I ought not to do anything unmanly because of the danger which I ran, and I have not changed my mind now. I would very much rather defend myself as I did, and die, than as you would have had me do, and live.

And once again:

But, my friends, I think that it is a much harder thing to escape from wickedness than from death; for wickedness is swifter than death. And now I, who am old and slow, have been overtaken by the slower pursuer: and my accusers, who are clever and swift, have been overtaken by the swifter pursuer, which is wickedness. And now I shall go hence, sentenced by you to death; and they will go hence, sentenced by truth to receive the penalty of wickedness and evil. And I abide by this award as well as they. Perhaps it was right for these things to be so: and I think that they are fairly measured.

A great climax. First the strange defendant sets forth in a calm, almost reflective manner, what has actually taken place. Next he maintains once more his standpoint. But then there appears suddenly in his words the judgment on the judgment, the judgment of truth and right on that of fortuitous power, and passes its final sentence.

What the judges have done will profit them nothing. They wanted to disarm the spirit by force, but they will not succeed. The spiritual struggle which Socrates has begun—with the object of ensuring that a deeper sense of responsibility shall prevail, that the things of everyday life shall be measured by truer standards, and that piety shall acquire new foundations in truth—will pursue its course. His disciples will continue his work.

> *For if you think that you will restrain men from reproaching you for your evil lives by putting them to death, you are very much mistaken. That way of escape is hardly possible, and it is not a good one. It is much better, and much easier, not to silence reproaches, but to make yourselves as perfect as you can. This is my parting prophecy to you who have condemned me.*

The Reply to the True Judges

He then turns to those who have voted for his acquittal, and it is like the closing of an intimate circle in which he, the aged master, now going to his death, is alone with the men who have by their verdict entered into an understanding not only with him, but with truth and justice too.

> *With you who have acquitted me I should like to converse touching this thing that has come to pass, while the authorities are busy, and before I go to the place where I have to die. So, I pray you, remain with me until I go hence: there is no reason why we should not converse with each other while it is possible. I wish to explain to you, as my friends, the meaning of what has befallen me.*

He wishes to interpret the moment—truly a "moment" in the pregnant sense of the word—a short hour, passing by in the stream of time, but one in which a decision of eternal import has been taken. He interprets it by speaking, from out of his personal life, words of which it is impossible to exaggerate the calmness, the nearness to those addressed, the remoteness from the others.

> *A wonderful thing has happened to me, judges—for you I am right in calling judges. The prophetic sign, which I am wont to receive from the divine voice, has been constantly with me all through my life till now, opposing me in quite small matters if I were not going to act rightly. And now you yourselves see what has happened to me; a thing which might be thought, and which is sometimes actually reckoned, the supreme evil. But the sign of God did not*

withstand me when I was leaving my house in the morning, nor when I was coming up hither to the Court, nor at any point in my speech, when I was going to say anything: though at other times it has often stopped me in the very act of speaking. But now, in this matter, it has never once withstood me, either in my words or my actions. I will tell you what I believe to be the reason of that. This thing that has come upon me must be a good: and those of us who think that death is an evil must needs be mistaken. I have a clear proof that that is so; for my accustomed sign would certainly have opposed me, if I had not been going to fare well.

It is wonderful how the religious, philosophical and human elements coalesce here into a perfect unity. He goes on to put the question concerning the nature of death more precisely, carefully distinguishing, just as he would do if he were sitting in the company of his disciples. First the alternative:

And if we reflect in another way we shall see that we may well hope that death is a good. For the state of death is one of two things: either the dead man wholly ceases to be, and loses all sensation; or, according to the common belief, it is a change and a migration of the soul into another place.

The first possibility:

And if death is the absence of all sensation, and like the sleep of one whose slumbers are unbroken by any dreams, it will be a wonderful gain. For if a man had to select that night in which he slept so soundly that he did not even see any dreams, and had to compare with it all the other nights and days of his life, and then had to say how many days and nights in his life he had spent better and more pleasantly than this night, I think that a private person, nay, even the great King himself, would find them easy to count, compared with the others. If that is the nature of death, I for one count it a gain. For then it appears that eternity is nothing more than a single night.

One seems almost to perceive weariness breaking out in the old man who has striven indefatigably all though his life: it would be wonderful to be able to sleep so soundly! But the matter is not left there, for the other possibility remains:

> But if death is a journey to another place, and the common belief be true, that there are all who have died, what good could be greater than this, my judges? Would a journey not be worth taking, at the end of which, in the other world, we should be released from the self-styled judges who are here, and should find the true judges, who are said to sit in judgment below, such as Minos, and Rhadamanthus, and Aeacus, and Triptolemus, and the other demi-gods who were just in their lives? Or what would you not give to converse with Orpheus and Musaeus and Hesiod and Homer? I am willing to die many times, if this be true. And for my own part I should have a wonderful interest in meeting there Palamedes, and Ajax the son of Telamon, and the other men of old who have died through an unjust judgment, and in comparing my experiences with theirs. That I think would be no small pleasure.

Here appears plainly that other court which was mentioned where Socrates stands before the Eternal in order that his person and work may be measured by eternal standards. He feels that he passes the test of these. Nay, this consciousness is even stronger. He says not only that he will find his purposes and work ratified in eternity, but that he will there continue the work he has been doing:

> And, above all, I could spend my time in examining those who are there, as I examine men here, and in finding out which of them is wise, and which of them thinks himself wise, when he is not wise. What would we not give, my judges, to be able to examine the leader of the great expedition against Troy, or Odysseus, or Sisyphus, or countless other men and women whom we could name? It would be an infinite happiness to converse with them, and to live with them, and to examine them. "Assuredly there they do not put men to death for doing that." For besides the other ways in which they are happier than we are, they are immortal, at least if the common belief be true.

We may note in passing what a vast self-assurance is expressed in these words. One day Socrates will be able to converse with the great ones of the past on that which is important, and only this intercourse will be truly adequate. Adequate to the importance of the subject, since only these partners have the requisite purity and power of insight; but adequate too to the claims of Socrates himself, who here on earth has always had to content himself with the inadequate. Socrates does not indeed mention this latter point expressly, but it is implied in the thought. One is reminded of the grand passage of the *Divine Comedy* where Dante meets the great men of antiquity in Limbo, is received by the five greatest poets into their circle, and is honoured with secret discourses "concerning which it is well to be silent" (*Inf.* iv. 82–105).

Socrates here transfers the cause of his condemnation into its idea. The court which has condemned him is, so to speak, metaphysically dissolved. Its work has come to nothing. In the form of mythological ideas Socrates becomes aware of his own work, and unites himself with its eternal pattern.

Then he comes back to the present:

And you too, judges, must face death with a good courage, and believe this as a truth, that no evil can happen to a good man, either in life, or after death. His fortunes are not neglected by the gods; and what has come to me to-day has not come by chance. I am persuaded that it was better for me to die now, and to be released from trouble: and that was the reason why the sign never turned me back. And so I am hardly angry with my accusers, or with those who have condemned me to die.

He does not mean by this to relieve his accusers of their responsibility. Their intentions were evil:

Yet it was not with this mind that they accused me and condemned me, but meaning to do me an injury. So far I may find fault with them.

What Socrates says about his accusers must not be overestimated. The question of true forgiveness does not arise. He is in fact not yet concerned with the problem of forgiveness at all. He achieves the very great merit of "not bearing his accusers any malice", because he is of the opinion that death is better than life. He overcomes, then, the hatred which springs from the immediate will to live against the enemy who threatens it with death—not, however, from the motive of a freedom which is able to see even this enemy as a man and to receive him into an ultimate relationship, but by virtue of an insight into the relation of life and death. It is a philosophical conquest; as such truly great, but no more than this.

Then comes a strange testament, full of irony:

Yet I have one request to make of them. When my sons grow up, visit them with punishment, my friends, and vex them in the same way that I have vexed you, if they seem to you to care for riches, or for any other thing, before virtue: and if they think that they are something, when they are nothing at all, reproach them, as I have reproached you, for not caring for what they should, and for thinking that they are great men when in fact they are worthless. And if you will do this, I myself and my sons will have received our deserts at your hands.

Finally the close, the last sentence, in which the character of Socrates emerges great and calm—and involuntarily one thinks with what feelings Plato's friends must have read this sentence:

But now the time has come, and we must go hence; I to die, and you to live. Whether life or death is better is known to God, and to God only.

Our enquiry seeks to discover how death is represented in the four dialogues with which we are concerned. To this question the *Apology* gives an important answer—particularly important because the personality of Socrates comes out so characteristically in it. What Socrates says in the first speech stands out against the background of the common view that death is the greatest evil. Socrates does not take death lightly, yet he does not fear it either. He knows values that are absolute and acknowledges claims of peremptory binding force; before these death becomes immaterial. Supreme among these is the divine commission as expressed in the oracle; but there is also the precept of fidelity to himself and the obligation imposed by his own honour. All this forbids him to make concessions to his judges' lust for power.

But the first speech already does more than merely maintain his own standpoint. No one knows, it says, whether death is really something evil and not rather perhaps something good. But the fact that the *Daimonion* has given no warning when Socrates was entering the court; that it has not interrupted him when he was about to say things in the course of his defence which made his situation worse: these are signs that death must be something good; for from the region whence the *Daimonion* speaks only what is ultimately good can come. It has already been remarked that there is at work in the manner of Socrates's defence a motive which is set on death. In a character of such a strong vitality and such positive intellectual clarity there can be no question of any morbid craving for death. Socrates does not wish for annihilation as such, but he knows that the final completion of his mission and of his existence can only be brought about through death. So this appears as a transition to the real. This is expressed quite clearly in the third speech, when he explains to the judges who have voted in his favour what has taken place in the events just concluded. Death there appears as a step to the true life. The mental picture of this does not derive merely from external faith, but is built on the inmost consciousness of his being and his mission. That which Socrates has done on earth, and because of which he must die, he will go on doing in the next life in a perfect and final manner. Not in the sense of primitive notions according to which the future life is a continuation of the present life freed from all defects, but in a spiritually purified sense: that which has taken place on earth in the venture of personal decision, beset with the contradictions of environment and jeopardized by the resistance of the temporal order, acquires in the next life its final significance. That Socrates is to converse with the heroes of old, compare his fate with theirs and interrogate them about theirs, means that his temporal activity is eternally ratified. This, then, is for his concrete existence something similar to what happens when in the process of cognition a thing enters into the light of the Idea: his earthly being and work is raised into the light of ultimate truth and allowed to rest there. Death appears as the transition thereto, and is recognized and accepted as such.

CRITO

PROLOGUE

IF WE ARRANGE the four dialogues concerning the death of Socrates in their proper order, not historical but logical, we notice in passing from one to the other a typical change of place, situation and mood. The *Euthyphro* takes place in the street, and the conversation arises from the chance meeting of two persons passing on their way. The *Apology* is enacted in a highly official place, before the supreme court of the state, which has to pronounce on the indictment against Socrates. Then, in the *Crito,* scene and action retire into tranquillity: Socrates is in prison, and his old friend comes and makes, in private conversation, a last attempt to induce him to escape. Finally the *Phaedo* is enacted in the same place; but now the circle of disciples is gathered round the master and he takes leave of them. The first text gives a kind of exposition of the whole. It displays the man and gives us to feel the conditions under which he will have to support the conflict that lies before him. The second gives the debate itself, and the reader shares the experience of its decision. In the third this decision is taken up again. Once more appears the possibility of evading death; so Socrates has one more opportunity of finally reviewing his decision and deliberately accepting its consequences. The fourth text, lastly, sets the whole in the light of eternity and shows the true issue.

The trial is long over. On that day the priest of Apollo had crowned the state ship which, according to ancient usage, sailed to Delos every year to thank the god there for the rescue of the Minotaur's victims, who had once sailed to Crete with Theseus. From the crowning to the return of the ship there was a truce of God in the city and no condemned person could be put to death. Adverse winds had delayed the voyage, so that Socrates had a long respite. But now travellers had arrived reporting that the homeward bound ship had reached Sunium and would soon be at Athens.

Meanwhile much had happened in the city. Many citizens had been on Socrates's side from the first. Others, who had voted against him, may in the meantime have seen the injustice of the sentence. In any case there is a strong body of opinion which expects the powerful friends of Socrates to help him to escape. The escape would certainly succeed, so the man would be saved and the tragedy averted. Those friends too have been working for this object and urging the prisoner, but he has always refused. It is now the eleventh hour.

> SOCR. *Why have you come at this hour, Crito? Is it not still early?*
> CRITO. *Yes, very early.*
> SOCR. *About what time is it?*
> CRITO. *It is just day-break.*
> SOCR. *I wonder that the jailor was willing to let you in.*
> CRITO. *He knows me now, Socrates, I come here so often; and besides, I have done him a service.*
> SOCR. *Have you been here long?*
> CRITO. *Yes; some time.*

The atmosphere is lively and intimate. Socrates sleeps calmly, although he knows that he may be wakened any morning with the news that the ship is approaching. Beside the bed sits Crito, of the same age as Socrates and his faithful friend; a simple warm-hearted character. Socrates now wakes up, and after the foregoing exchange of words asks:

> *Then why did you sit down without speaking? why did you not wake me at once?*
> CRITO. *Indeed, Socrates, I wish that I myself were not so sleepless and sorrowful. But I have been wondering to see how sweetly you sleep. And I purposely did not wake you, for I was anxious not to disturb your repose. Often before, all through your life, I have thought that your temper was a happy one; and I think so*

more than ever now, when I see how easily and calmly you bear the calamity that has come to you.

Socr. Nay, Crito, it would be absurd if at my age I were angry at having to die.

Crito. Other men as old are overtaken by similar calamities, Socrates; but their age does not save them from being angry with their fate.

Crito does not yet understand; so Socrates bids him first say what has brought him here:

But tell me, why are you here so early?

Crito. I am the bearer of bitter news, Socrates; not bitter, it seems, to you; but to me, and to all your friends, both bitter and grievous: and to none of them, I think, is it more grievous than to me.

Socr. What is it? Has the ship come from Delos, at the arrival of which I am to die?

Crito. No, it has not actually arrived: but I think that it will be here to-day, from the news which certain persons have brought from Sunium, who left it there. It is clear from their news that it will be here to-day; and then, Socrates, to-morrow your life will have to end.

Socr. Well, Crito, may it end fortunately.

But he thinks that the ship will not arrive at Athens yet. This conviction is the result of a dream which he had at the moment when his friend found him sleeping:

But I do not think that the ship will be here to-day.

Crito. Why do you suppose not?

Socr. I will tell you. I am to die on the day after the ship arrives, am I not?

Crito. That is what the authorities say.

Socr. Then I do not think that it will come to-day, but to-morrow. I judge from a certain dream which I saw a little while ago in the night: so it seems to be fortunate that you did not wake me.

CRITO. *And what was this dream?*

SOCR. *A fair and comely woman, clad in white garments seemed to come to me, and call me and say, "O Socrates— 'The third day hence shalt thou fair Phthia reach'."*[1]

CRITO. *What a strange dream, Socrates!*

SOCR. *But its meaning is clear; at least to me, Crito.*

CRITO. *Yes, too clear, it seems.*

It is high time then. So Crito tries once more, with all his eloquence, to induce his friend to escape. If Socrates dies, his friend is lost to him; people will say too that he has done nothing to save him. And yet it would all be so easy. Money and helping hands are in readiness. The danger from the authorities is not too great. Abroad he will find helpers everywhere, especially in Thessaly, where Crito has trusty guest-friends. His children too will be benefited, for they will still have their father and will be sure of a good education:

Take care, Socrates, lest these things be not evil only, but also dishonourable to you and to us. Consider then; or rather the time for consideration is past; we must resolve; and there is only one plan possible. Everything must be done to-night. If we delay any longer, we are lost.

A long speech, full of urgent anxiety; wholly unphilosophical, wholly turned towards the practical, the expression of the true, warm heart of a friend. It compels Socrates to undertake the final review of his position.

The case has already been decided before the civil court. It is now, through the favour of circumstances and the activity of friends, brought up for discussion once more before the inner tribunal, that of conscience. A peculiar solitariness marks the conversation. Socrates conducts it with Crito—in truth he is conducting it with himself.

[1] *Iliad IX*, 363.

THE PROBLEM AND ITS DISCUSSION

The Theme

THE FIRST sentences go straight to the centre of the problem:

> SOCR. *My dear Crito, if your anxiety to save me be right, it is most valuable: but if it be not right, its greatness makes it all the more dangerous. We must consider then whether we are to do as you say, or not.*

Two regions are distinguished: the immediate reality with its danger for a friend's life, and the moral standard with its binding validity for conscience. The decision must be taken in the second region; and it must be all the more absolute because Socrates has throughout his life proclaimed the absoluteness of duty.

> *For I am still what I always have been, a man who will listen to no voice but the voice of the reasoning[1] which on consideration I find to be truest. I cannot cast aside my former arguments because this misfortune has come to me. They seem to me to be as true as ever they were, and I hold exactly the same ones in honour and esteem as I used to: and if we have no better reasoning to substitute for them, I certainly shall not agree to your proposal, not even though the power of the multitude should scare us with fresh terrors, as children are scared with hobgoblins, and inflict upon us new fines and imprisonments, and deaths.*

The discussion is to start from what Crito himself has said; he has spoken indeed of the opinion of people who will reproach him if he has not helped his friend:

> *How then shall we most fitly examine the question? Shall we go back first to what you say about the opinions of men, and ask if we used to be right in thinking that we ought to pay attention to some*

---

[1] *Logos* means the structure of the spoken words, the "speech" or the "sentence"; at the same time it means also the structure of the thoughts expressed therein, the developed intellectual significance.

opinions, and not to others? Used we to be right in saying so before I was condemned to die, and has it now become apparent that we were talking at random, and arguing for the sake of argument, and that it was really nothing but play and nonsense?

The question is put very urgently, and Socrates goes on immediately to formulate it a second and yet a third time:

Consider then: do you not think it reasonable to say that we should not esteem all the opinions of men, but only some, nor the opinions of all men, but only of some men? What do you think? Is not this true?
CRITO. *It is.*
SOCR. *And we should esteem the good opinions, and not the worthless ones?*
CRITO. *Yes.*
SOCR. *But the good opinions are those of the wise, and the worthless ones those of the foolish?*
CRITO. *Of course.*

THE OPINIONS OF MEN

When a man wants to give his body proper care and exercise, he will not "pay attention to every man's praise and blame and opinion", but to that of "one man only, namely one who is a doctor or teacher of physical culture". If he does not do that, he suffers injury in the matter in question, namely the health and fitness of his body. One must act in the same way when "it is a question of justice and injustice, the base and the noble, the good and the bad, all of which is the subject of our present talk". Here, too, we must not "follow the opinion of the crowd and fear it", but "only that of the one man, if there is one, who is skilled in the matter, and whom we must fear and beware of more than all others put together". If we do not do this, we suffer injury in that part of us which "is benefited by justice, but ruined by injustice"—namely the soul, which lives on the good, just as the body lives on the things which make it grow. And it is pointed out with all emphasis that this is a question of life and death (47a–d).

> Socr. *Now, if, by listening to the opinions of those who do not understand, we disable that part of us which is improved by health and crippled by disease, is our life worth living, when it is crippled? It is the body, is it not?*
> Crito. *Yes.*
> Socr. *Is life worth living with the body crippled and in a bad state?*
> Crito. *No, certainly not.*
> Socr. *Then is life worth living when that part of us which is maimed by wrong and benefited by right is crippled?*

"No" is the answer to be supplied. And it is just as serious as in the case of the body:

> *Or do we consider that part of us, whatever it is, which has to do with right and wrong to be of less consequence than our body?*
> Crito. *No, certainly not.*
> Socr. *But more valuable?*
> Crito. *Yes, much more so.*
> Socr. *Then, my excellent friend, we must not think so much of what the many will say of us; we must think of what the one man, who understands right and wrong, and of what Truth herself will say of us. And so you are mistaken to begin with, when you invite us to regard the opinion of the multitude concerning the right and the honourable and the good, and their opposites. But, it may be said, the multitude can put us to death?*
> Crito. *Yes, that is evident. That may be said, Socrates.*

The decision, then, lies not in what is quantitative—power and success—but in what is qualitative—truth, justice, the good and the noble. But in order to make clear the essential differences between the two orders—that of the immediately real and powerful on the one hand, and that of the valid and right on the other—the many, who can compel and destroy, are set up as supporters of the first, and of the second the few, nay "the one": the actual extreme case, where it is defenceless and stands only on principle.

What follows takes the thought further:

> Socr. *True. But, my excellent friend, to me it appears that the conclusion which we have just reached, is the same as our conclusion*

of former times. Now consider whether we still hold to the belief, that we should set the highest value, not on living, but on living well?

CRITO. *Yes, we do.*

SOCR. *And living well and honourably and rightly mean the same thing: do we hold to that or not?*

CRITO. *We do.*

From this appears the conclusion for Socrates's own case:

SOCR. *Then, starting from these premises, we have to consider whether it is right or not right for me to try to escape from prison, without the consent of the Athenians. If we find that it is right, we will try: if not, we will let it alone.*

This is underlined by the proud sentences:

I am afraid that considerations of expense, and of reputation, and of bringing up my children, of which you talk, Crito, are only the reflections of our friends, the many, who lightly put men to death, and who would, if they could, as lightly bring them to life again, without a thought. But reason, which is our guide, shows us that we can have nothing to consider but the question which I asked just now: namely, shall we be doing right if we give money and thanks to the men who are to aid me in escaping, and if we ourselves take our respective parts in my escape? Or shall we in truth be doing wrong, if we do all this? And if we find that we should be doing wrong, then we must not take any account either of death, or of any other evil that may be the consequence of remaining quietly here, but only of doing wrong.

THE ABSOLUTENESS OF THE CLAIM

And now the unconditional nature of the claim of the true, the just, the good, the beautiful—in a word, of that which is valid by virtue of its meaning—is worked out. The maxim that no injustice may be done is valid, in whatever situation a man may be, and whatever consequences may result for him:

SOCR. *Ought we never to do wrong intentionally at all; or may we do wrong in some ways, and not in others? Or, as we have often agreed in former times, is it never either good or honourable to*

> do wrong? Have all our former conclusions been forgotten in these few days? Old men as we were, Crito, did we not see, in days gone by, when we were gravely conversing with each other, that we were no better than children? Or is not what we used to say most assuredly the truth, whether the world agrees with us or not? Is not wrong-doing an evil and a shame to the wrong-doer in every case, whether we incur a heavier or a lighter punishment than death as the consequence of doing right? Do we believe that?
>
> CRITO. *We do.*

The maxim admits of no restriction, even when one's neighbour does not acknowledge it.

> SOCR. *Neither, if we ought never to do wrong at all, ought we to repay wrong with wrong, as the world thinks we may?*
> CRITO. *Clearly not.*

The validity and binding force of the good does not depend on how the other man—we may conclude further, how any man at all—behaves in practice. It does not derive from contingent resources and eventualities, but from the nature of the good itself, regardless of what is done or omitted anywhere. A tremendous perception: and one feels the excitement that accompanies it. With it ancient thought touches the limit of its possibilities.

The inference is fraught with peril. The man who reasons thus leaves behind the safeguard that lies in regard for consequences. He acknowledges that which is valid in itself, the order of which by no means coincides with that of concrete events. He places himself under the claim of the absolute, while he continues to live on in the realm of the factual and relative, which does not necessarily conform to that claim. Thereby he exposes himself to the consequences which arise from the conflict—and indeed Socrates warns his friend:

> *Then we ought not to repay wrong with wrong or do harm to any man, no matter what we may have suffered from him. And in conceding this, Crito, be careful that you do not concede more than you mean.*

This is where the ways part:

For I know that only a few men hold, or ever will hold this opinion. And those who so hold it, and those who do not, have no common ground of argument; they can of necessity only look with contempt on each other's belief.

So it is a momentous decision:

Do you therefore consider very carefully whether you agree with me and share my opinion. Are we to start in our inquiry from the doctrine that it is never right either to do wrong, or to repay wrong with wrong, or to avenge ourselves on any man who harms us, by harming him in return? Or do you disagree with me and dissent from my principle? I myself have believed in it for a long time, and I believe in it still. But if you differ in any way, explain to me how. If you still hold to our former opinion, listen to my next point.

The last phase of the conversation is important for the problem of the whole enquiry. In it comes out the primal philosophical experience of validity, according to which the valid—here taken as an ethical norm—is self-subsistent, independent of all empirical conditions, and can be recognized as such. It is experienced in its extreme case, where it endangers the life of the percipient, and he acknowledges it in the sacrifice of that life.

But there is something else too in these sentences. The manner in which Socrates makes clear the absoluteness of this validity is more than a mere matter of demonstrating and teaching; it is rather a penetration of this validity, an embracing of it, taking stand on it and taking root in it. It is an existential process, and one of the most real events of the Socratic-Platonic world: the process by which the mind ascertains the absolute which appears in truth. And not merely so as to say "It is so", but rather: "In that I perceive and say that it is so, something happens to me who say it. In perceiving that it not only is so, but cannot be otherwise, I am myself freed from the changeable and contingent and secured in what is definitive." To perceive the absolute means not only to contemplate the worthiest object, but oneself, in virtue of one's being, to share in the absoluteness of this object. The enquiry here hurries ahead; for it is not until we come to interpret the *Phaedo* that it will become quite clear that this is Plato's view. But the situation which will unfold there in its full significance is already present in its rudiments here. Socrates knows that he must die if he affirms the absoluteness of the moral norm. But the fervour with which he makes the affirmation, and which breaks out at the close of the dialogue in the phrases about the sound of flutes and the Corybantic ecstasy, shows how closely related in him are the affirmation of the absolute and readiness to die—so closely, indeed, that death is overcome in that affirmation.

The Final Inference

The reader feels a kind of caesura: what has been said before is brought out in all its significance, so that, being fully acknowledged, it may afford a groundwork for the decisive logical steps which are coming.

> CRITO. *Yes, I hold to it, and I agree with you. Go on.*
> SOCR. *Then, my next point, or rather my next question, is this: Ought a man to perform his just agreements, or may he shuffle out of them?*
> CRITO. *He ought to perform them.*

The good, which must be done under all circumstances, is conceived here in a special way, namely as fulfilment of an agreed contractual obligation. This leads on to the following passage, in which is expressed the relation of the Platonic man to the State —which is the *polis*, the city, a community of limited dimensions and therefore capable of being vividly present to the consciousness. This passage tells the story of the meeting with the Laws.

The laws are the way in which justice is realized in the State. The meaning of "justice" in the Platonic sense will only be fully developed in the *Republic*: it is the right ordering of life, as resulting from the nature of things, the Ideas. The concrete formula for the relation of the individual State to the Idea is expressed by its laws. They indicate the extent to which the Idea permeates it. They embody the will of the community to realize the Idea. With respect to the individual, therefore, they are the advocates of right order, the representatives of the Idea. Socrates says now:

> *Consider it in this way. Suppose the laws and the commonwealth[1] were to come and appear to me as I was preparing to run away (if that is the right phrase to describe my escape) and were to ask, "Tell us, Socrates, what have you in your mind to do?"*

The story is more than a mere allegory, for these "shapes of Law" have a lifelike quality, present and powerful, so that something like a breath of mysticism pervades the words. They reveal the citizen's relation to his native *polis*—the emotional element, and also the categorical element, if one may call it so, which is contained in it. And the Laws in fact accost the man at the moment when he is about to leave the city: that is, at the critical moment of final decision, when the possibility of negation brings into consciousness the entire energy of the positive sense. They come before him as objective beings, almost as the tutelary deities of the State; and they are answered from the depths of conscience.

These Laws ask:
> *"What do you mean by trying to escape, but to destroy us the laws, and the whole city, so far as in you lies? Do you think that a state can exist and not be overthrown, in which the decisions of law are of no force, and are disregarded and set at nought by private individuals?"*

What answer will Socrates have?
> *Shall I reply, "But the state has injured me: it has decided my cause wrongly." Shall we say that?*
>
> CRITO. *Certainly we will, Socrates.*

The sentences are characteristic of the two interlocutors. Even Crito, the practical man, living entirely by the feeling of the moment, has a relation to *polis* and *nomos*; but he takes them in a thoroughly

---
[1] "*To koinon*," that which is in common; perhaps even that which belongs to the entirety.

realistic fashion, from the point of view of *do ut des*. He has just admitted that one may not do injustice to any man, even when one has suffered injustice from him; but he has already forgotten that— for the reason that it never amounted to real understanding for him. He now speaks according to his real sentiments, taking the State and its laws as powers which the individual will-to-live confronts as an equal. Socrates feels differently. The laws do not merely exist, but are valid, and that puts them into an order quite different from that of the individual will. They say that the sentence which has been legally passed must be carried out, and that this is "justice". The possibility that the law itself may be at fault and require to be tested by the appropriate standard, namely the Idea of law; that consequently the individual derives hence a true right to criticism and resistance, in which lies indeed the antecedent condition both for human freedom and for the progress of the juridical order as such—this possibility is simply not taken into consideration. Law derives from the authority of the State. It is clear that the individual may not on his own authority annul a penalty which follows from the application of the law. The question here, however, is whether he may withdraw from the consequences of an unreasonable and unjust sentence; and it is very characteristic of the general tendency of the fate of Socrates and its presentation by Plato that this question is not seriously raised, although it could easily have been raised from the Platonic starting-point. We meet once again with that peculiar radicalizing tendency which has already shown itself in the *Apology:* the inward determination that the outcome shall be a tragic one. There is something in Socrates making for death, regardless of whether that involves fastening the burden of injustice on the State, which he nevertheless champions so wholeheartedly. Not to see this is to take the whole thing in a merely aesthetic way and to place the fascination of tragic sequence above the truth. This means coming into conflict with Plato himself, and perhaps even more so with Socrates; for they are concerned not with the unfolding of a great character or a tragic situation, but with the question: What is true, and what ought one to do?

Then begins the actual dialogue between the "Laws" and the man who is about to evade their claim. They say:

> "Socrates, wonder not at our words, but answer us; you yourself are accustomed to ask questions and to answer them. What complaint have you against us and the city, that you are trying to destroy us? Are we not, first, your parents? Through us your father took your mother and begat you. Tell us, have you any fault to find with those of us that are the laws of marriage?" "I have none," I should reply. "Or have you any fault to find with those of us that regulate the nurture and education of the child, which you, like others, received? Did we not do well in bidding your father educate you in music and gymnastic?" "You did," I should say.

There is a close relation between the laws and the individual. Socrates has affirmed this relation at many decisive junctures of his life. He has recognized it as the guarantor of his own well-being; this involves consequences.

> "Well then, since you were brought into the world and nurtured and educated by us, how, in the first place, can you deny that you are our child and our slave, as your fathers were before you?"

By so doing, he has entered into a relation of dependence and subjection to them. So he stands before them, not on equal terms, but as before superior authorities and higher powers. He cannot, therefore, oppose his judgment to them as equal to equal, but must submit, even if he thinks he is suffering injustice.

> "And if this be so, do you think that your rights are on a level with ours? Do you think that you have a right to retaliate upon us if we should try to do anything to you? You had not the same rights that your father had, or that your master would have had, if you had been a slave. You had no right to retaliate upon them if they ill-treated you, or to answer them if they reviled you, or to strike them back if they struck you, or to repay them evil with evil in any way. And do you think that you may retaliate on your country and its laws? If we try to destroy you, because we think it right, will you in return do all that you can to destroy us, the laws, and your country, and say that in so doing you are doing right, you, the man, who in truth thinks so much of virtue?"

D

Indeed the authority of the State is even greater than that of father or mother:

> "*Or are you too wise to see that your country is worthier, and more august, and more sacred, and holier, and held in higher honour both by the gods and by all men of understanding, than your father and your mother and all your other ancestors; and that is your bounden duty to reverence it, and to submit to it, and to approach it more humbly than you would approach your father, when it is angry with you; and either to do whatever it bids you to do or to persuade it to excuse you; and to obey in silence if it orders you to endure stripes or imprisonment, or if it send you to battle to be wounded or to die? That is what is your duty. You must not give way, nor retreat, nor desert your post. In war, and in the court of justice, and everywhere, you must do whatever your city and your country bid you do, or you must convince them that their commands are unjust. But it is against the law of God to use violence to your father or to your mother; and much more so is it against the law of God to use violence to your country."*[1]

After forgoing criticism of the law itself—not from any individual or casual opinion, from a *doxa*, but from genuine *noêsis*, from insight into the Idea—the result cannot run otherwise than it does:

> *What answer shall we make, Crito? Shall we say that the laws speak truly, or not?*
> CRITO. *I think that they do.*

He assents; how far he is convinced—and not merely in his understanding, which has probably long been accustomed to bow to the superior dialectic of his philosophical friend, but in his honest heart's feeling for reality and sense—is undecided. We for our part cannot but think that the question of the relation between law and the individual, authority and conscience, is not pushed to

---

[1] When Euthyphro says at the beginning of the dialogue that he is going to sue his father, Socrates is horrified and sees in this an impiety. The words of the "Laws" make clear the ideas and sentiments that lie behind this attitude.

the ultimate reaches of the problem. The dialogue however—just as the *Apology*—is concerned not with this problem, but with the existential sense of the great and unique man Socrates. He has, in an understanding with the deity which is in the end clear to him alone, acknowledged the laws of Athens as the executive agents of his fate. For him therefore it is a matter of more than mere moral duty. He stands for something new, which imperils the traditional; he is therefore bound all the more strictly to all that is valid, in a kind of atoning justice which at the same time preserves him from arbitrariness. It cannot forbid him to tell the truth; in this, as expressly declared in the *Apology*, he must obey the divine voice, even if he transgresses the laws in so doing. But in all that does not concern this ultimate, they bind him more strictly than others, precisely because he is the servant of such a revolution. And perhaps, over and above this, there is caught a hint of that other "law" according to which the revelation of that which is higher must be paid for by him who brings it, and this higher good is incorporated into history in the same measure in which the price is paid.

The Laws can adduce even more reasons. Socrates continues:

> "*Then consider, Socrates,*" *perhaps they would say,* "*if we are right in saying that by attempting to escape you are attempting to injure us. We brought you into the world, we nurtured you, we educated you, we gave you and every other citizen a share of all the good things we could. Yet we proclaim that if any man of the Athenians is dissatisfied with us, he may take his goods and go away whithersoever he pleases: we give that permission to every man who chooses to avail himself of it, so soon as he has reached man's estate, and sees us, the laws, and the administration of our city. No one of us stands in his way or forbids him to take his goods and go wherever he likes, whether it be to an Athenian colony, or to any foreign country, if he is dissatisfied with us and with the city. But we say that every man of you who remains here, seeing how we administer justice, and how we govern the city in other matters, has agreed, by the very fact of remaining here, to do whatsoever we bid him. And, we say, he who disobeys us does a threefold*

wrong: he disobeys us who are his parents, and he disobeys us who fostered him, and he disobeys us after he has agreed to obey us, without persuading us that we are wrong."

Then a kind of smiling humanity plays over all this seriousness, when Socrates says that the Laws would catch him above all others with these arguments. For they would say that he, even more than others, had declared himself in agreement with them.

> They would say, "Socrates, we have very strong evidence that you were satisfied with us and with the city. You would not have been content to stay at home in it more than other Athenians, unless you had been satisfied with it more than they. You never went away from Athens to the festivals, save once to the Isthmian games, nor elsewhere except on military service; you never made other journeys like other men; you had no desire to see other cities or other laws; you were contented with us and our city. So strongly did you prefer us, and agree to be governed by us: and what is more, you begat children in this city, you found it so pleasant."

We seem to see him before us in the flesh, living in the city, in spirit raised above what is earthly, and yet so intimately conversant with it. We see him pledged to the highest, but knowing too the ins and outs of everything, and interesting himself in the most ordinary affairs of life; assuredly well-informed about everything that goes on in country and city and street, and perhaps not even averse from a bit of gossip—this man "truly touched of Dionysus", in whose heart the *Daimonion* speaks, and who yet at the same time has about him such a funny bourgeois air of pedantic rationalism that one often wonders how his disciple Plato, the aristocrat and great artist, could have put up with his constant company.

> SOCR. Then they would say, "Are you not breaking your covenants and agreements with us? And you were not led to make them by force or by fraud: you had not to make up your mind in a hurry. You had seventy years in which you might have gone away, if you had been dissatisfied with us, or if the agreement had seemed to you unjust. But you preferred neither Lacedaemon nor Crete,

though you are fond of saying that they are well governed, nor any other state, either of the Hellenes, or the Barbarians. You went away from Athens less than the lame and the blind and the cripple. Clearly you, far more than other Athenians, were satisfied with the city, and also with us who are its laws: for who would be satisfied with a city which had no laws?"

If Socrates really goes away, he will find himself in an impossible situation:

"For yourself, you might go to one of the neighbouring cities, to Thebes or to Megara for instance—for both of them are well governed—but, Socrates, you will come as an enemy to these commonwealths; and all who care for their city will look askance at you, and think that you are a subverter of law. And you will confirm the judges in their opinion, and make it seem that their verdict was a just one. For a man who is a subverter of law, may well be supposed to be a corrupter of the young and thoughtless. Then will you avoid well-governed states and civilised men? Will life be worth having, if you do? Or will you consort with such men, and converse without shame—about what, Socrates? About the things which you talk of here? Will you tell them that virtue, and justice, and institutions, and law are the most precious things that men can have? And do you not think that that will be a shameful thing in Socrates?"

Finally the deduction from this:

"No, Socrates, be advised by us who have fostered you. Think neither of children, nor of life, nor of any other thing before justice, that when you come to the other world you may be able to make your defence before the rulers who sit in judgment there."

And the last grand proof:

"Now you will go away wronged, not by us, the laws, but by men. But if you repay evil with evil, and wrong with wrong in this shameful way, and break your agreements and covenants with us,

and injure those whom you should least injure, yourself, and your friends, and your country, and us, and so escape, then we shall be angry with you while you live, and when you die our brethren, the laws in Hades, will not receive you kindly; for they will know that on earth you did all that you could to destroy us. Listen then to us, and let not Crito persuade you to do as he says."

The *Apology* has already combined an earthly activity with one beyond the grave—in the passage where Socrates says that part of the happiness of the next life will consist in raising what he has done here to its eternal significance. Something similar happens here: the laws which must be obeyed on earth are conceived as parallel with those of the next world. Valid action is eternal action; and eternal not only in meaning, but also in being.

CONCLUSION

The conclusion of the whole is short and sublime:

Know well, my dear friend Crito, that this is what I seem to hear, as the worshippers of Cybele seem, in their frenzy, to hear the music of flutes: and the sound of these words rings loudly in my ears, and drowns all other words. And I feel sure that if you try to change my mind you will speak in vain; nevertheless, if you think that you will succeed, say on.

CRITO. *I can say no more, Socrates.*

SOCR. *Then let it be, Crito: and let us do as I say, seeing that God so directs us.*

The decision which had been expressed in the great speeches before the court has now, in face of the possibility of evading it, once more been reviewed in quiet conversation with the old friend of Socrates's youth. Except at the beginning, where Crito announces the news of the ship's approach and explains how urgent the situation has become, he hardly takes part in a real conversation, but merely adds his "Yes" and "Of course" to the monologue which Socrates is conducting with himself—or rather to that dialogue which is going on between the inexorable inspector of human opinions and "the Laws".

The voyage of the festal ship has been delayed; so Socrates has spent a very long time in prison. The confinement is not rigorous, his disciples and friends have easy access to him, and the days will have passed for the most part in their customary conversation. Socrates, however, is not only the philosopher of the absolute demand of the true and the good, but also a man of strong and, despite his advanced age, unbroken vitality. So he will have had times in which life has raised its voice, and he has had to withstand it. From this point of view the duologue of the *Crito* seems like the uttering aloud of previous reflections in private.

The demand of the good has now attained the incontrovertibility of rational evidence—and at the same time the peace-giving power which religious experience has over the mind. The divinity which presides over Socrates's life is, as the *Apology* has shown, and the *Phaedo* will show again, Apollo. It is he who speaks in the *Daimonion's* warning as well as in the Pythian oracle. But with the words about the sound of flutes and the ecstasy of Corybants the experience passes for a moment from the realm of his brightness into that of Dionysiac enthusiasm—with regard to which we must not forget, of course, that Apollo and Dionysus are in reality nearer to one another than the usual antithesis supposes.

Like the *Apology*, the *Crito* shows the connection that exists between the problem of death and that of conscience. To overcome death is to discover in it a meaning which inserts it into the significant whole of life. This meaning lies for the Platonic Socrates in the mind's relation to the true and good, in the relation of the conscience to that which ought to be. In spite of the last sentences of the dialogue, the victory has not a Dionysiac character. That would be the case if death were understood as the ebbing of life's wave, followed by a new surge from the great stream; or as the culmination of life, in which the whole, shattering the individual form, breaks triumphantly through. Rather, death is overcome by the spiritually awakening man's becoming aware of an absolute which stands on the other side of life's stream and its rhythms, of birth as of death: by his becoming aware of the Just, the True, the

Holy or Good. In its presence he experiences a peculiar obligation, proceeding from the nature of validity itself—but also, necessarily connected with this, something ultimate inside himself which has the faculty of responding to that validity and being bound by it: conscience. It is specifically related to that indestructible validity.

By this experience all that is transient is deprived of its power, and a security won which can no more be shaken. In the *Euthyphro* it is still latent. It shows itself more in that which fails and is found wanting than in what is positively gained. Euthyphro is completely wrapped up in what is transitory, and breaks down before all Socrates's demands; it is clear from this very fact that the latter's existence is differently based, even though this difference does not attain expression. In the *Apology* the Socratic consciousness of being bound by the valid breaks out forcibly. Not as an overpowering by something numinous, nor as an inundation by some kind of mysterious life, which might equally well be sublimated vitality; but as a commitment in full insight and freedom. What is grasped thereby is conscience. The same experience of conscience recurs in the *Crito*, only more inward and tranquil. The broad publicity of the law-court, with its passions and strifes, has disappeared; Socrates stands before his friend only. But this friend is not capable of actually conducting the dialogue; it takes place in Socrates himself, between the will-to-live of his strong, rich nature and his conscience. In the heart of this dialogue an almost uncanny scene is enacted. On the road which leads from Athens abroad a fleeing Socrates is met and addressed by the Laws of his native city, the embodiment of what the present hour demands; and it is wonderful with what sincerity their claim is answered by conscience —that most inward and at the same time most remote thing in man, which can discern the voice of validity through all the bustle of life. It is intimated here that there is something in man himself which is correlated to the laws and comprised in their fulfilment. The *Phaedo* finally lifts the whole relation to its ultimate clarity. It understands conscience as the organ for the significance and majesty of the valid in general—not only for the morally good, but also for the true. That the morally good and the true are severally and together anchored in the Good of holiness, and that conscience is the inmost response of living man to the eternal claim, constitutes the breadth of the Platonic spirit. With these thoughts the *Phaedo*, which of course belongs to the mature period of Plato's work, rises above the foregoing dialogues; but it adds nothing foreign to them, it only brings their basic principle to its final fulfilment.

PHAEDO

THE ARRANGEMENT OF THE DIALOGUE

THE *Phaedo* is the longest and most difficult of the four dialogues with which we are concerned; before analysing it in detail, therefore, we will glance at the construction and arrangement of the whole.

The dialogue proper is preceded by a preliminary scene. Echecrates of Phlius meets Phaedo, a disciple of Socrates, and asks him to tell him about the last hours of his master. Phaedo is very ready to comply.

He first relates how, owing to the late return of the festal ship, the execution of the sentence has been delayed, and what happened on the very last day in the prison—to begin with, up to the moment when Socrates's wife, Xanthippe, with their youngest little son, has taken leave of her husband and been led out (57a–60c).

Then follow the actual conversations in the circle of Socrates's disciples, who also have arrived there (60c–115a). In these can be distinguished further an introduction and three main parts.

The introduction develops out of a message from Socrates to the poet Evenus, bidding the latter follow him as soon as possible. It proposes the thesis that the life of a philosopher is simply nothing else but a preparation for death, or even is itself a continual dying. From this results the theme of the principal conversation: for such a conception of philosophy can only have sense if something in the philosopher survives death. Is that the case? Is the soul immortal? (60c–70c).

The proof that it is so is given by Socrates in conversation with Cebes and Simmias, two of the circle. He proves it first—in the first part of the dialogue—by taking death as the dialectically correlative process to being born, and relates them both to an essential substratum, namely the indestructible soul. Thereby death appears as a phase in a comprehensive whole, and is made relative. The same conclusion results from interpreting knowledge as reminiscence:

for it follows thence that what remembers itself, the soul, must have existed before birth. But if that is so—and the thought is here linked with the preceding argument—the soul must also persist beyond death (70c–77a).

The doubt is expressed whether the latter inference really follows; and this leads to a brief interlude, in which Socrates encourages his friends to go on seeking truth even when he is dead (77a–78a).

Then begins the second part of the main dialogue, with a new train of thought. Only that can die which is composite, that is to say, corporeal; but what is simple, that is, spiritual, is indissoluble. The Idea is absolutely indissoluble; but it is shown that the human soul is related to the Idea and must therefore be indestructible likewise. It is fundamentally so by its nature; but according to its individual character it becomes so in proportion as it attains to pure knowledge, thereby detaching itself from the corporeal and assimilating itself to the Idea (78b–84b).

Thereupon follows a marked break, a second interlude. Socrates's arguments have made a deep impression on everybody. Cebes and Simmias, however, are not yet convinced, and Socrates encourages them to speak. The former is of the opinion that what has been said only proves that the soul survives a particular body, not that it necessarily survives all bodies in the course of its reincarnations. The second critic conjectures that the soul is perhaps nothing else but the harmony of the body and must therefore perish with the body's parts. The objections turn the emotion into bewilderment, and this communicates itself also to the hearer of the account, Echecrates, with the result that the prison scene is again brought clearly before the mind. This makes the effect all the more vivid when Phaedo tells how Socrates heartens his friends and leads them back to the problem (84c–91c).

Here begins the third and most important part of the main discourse. Socrates first refutes Simmias' objection, by analysing the relation in which the soul stands to the body, especially its conflict with the latter's instincts, from which it follows that it cannot be the function of the body. In his answer to Cebes he then finds the essence of the soul in the fact that it stands to the Idea of Life in a relation of necessity, which excludes death; hence it cannot die. These arguments form the climax of the whole dialogue (91c–107b).

It ends with a practical consequence: If the soul is of such a nature and dignity, it must be treated with corresponding care—a duty which is corroborated by a mythological description of the mansions of the future life (107c–115a).

The close of the dialogue takes us back to the introduction and narrates the Master's death (115b–118a).

INTRODUCTION

The Setting

In the other three works the dialogue begins at once and introduces the reader directly to the situation; here it is embedded in a conversation between two men which takes place after all is over. This procedure has, firstly, a literary advantage: the author can bring before the reader events as well as conversations, and can depict the situation more fully than would be possible in a mere dialogue. But there is a further consideration. If the reader does not forget the introductory scene, but keeps it, as he should, before him all through as the determining element—Plato himself suggests this when, before the decisive arguments, he makes Phaedo describe the bewilderment which seizes everyone after the objections of Cebes and Simmias, and the same impression comes over Echecrates as he listens to the description—then he will feel how much greater reverence is shown by reproducing the tenor of just this dialogue from memory, than by presenting it directly. And one last point. The fact that the occurrence of this death and the picture of the man who underwent it rise out of memory, gives Socrates the place he holds in Platonic thought as a whole. Phaedo says: "I will try to relate it. Nothing is more pleasant to me than to recall Socrates to my mind, whether by speaking of him myself, or by listening to others."—"Indeed, Phaedo," answers Echecrates, "you will have an audience like yourself." The figure and its fate are taken straight from the present and raised to the timeless.

It is all very solemn. The conversation takes place not in private, as in the Crito, where the final decision is made between the tempter-friend and Socrates, but in a wide circle and at an official hour, so to speak. Not, however, in a strange, unfriendly publicity, as in the *Apology* before the court, but among friends and disciples, more intimately bound to the Master than wife and child. Officials cross the room: the Eleven, who loose the prisoner's fetters on the last day, to give him freedom of movement when he takes the step to death. The great religious festival with which the State, according to ancient tradition, celebrates the exploits of Theseus and the favour of the gods, penetrates even the prison doors. The State ship, which is sent every year to Delos in thanksgiving to Apollo, has returned. Socrates must now die, having enjoyed a reprieve during its voyage, which has been prolonged by adverse winds. So round the jail opens the wide space of the Aegean Sea and the glorious sunlight of Hellas.

> ECHECRATES. *We were rather surprised to find that he did not die till so long after the trial. Why was that, Phaedo?*
>
> PHAEDO. *It was an accident, Echecrates. The stern of the ship, which the Athenians send to Delos, happened to have been crowned on the day before the trial.*
>
> ECH. *And what is this ship?*
>
> PHAEDO. *It is the ship, as the Athenians say, in which Theseus took the seven youths and the seven maidens to Crete, and saved them from death, and himself was saved. The Athenians made a vow then to Apollo, the story goes, to send a sacred mission to Delos every year, if they should be saved; and from that time to this they have always sent it to the god, every year. They have a law to keep the city pure as soon as the mission begins, and not to execute any sentence of death until the ship has returned from Delos; and sometimes, when it is detained by contrary winds, that is a long while. The sacred mission begins when the priest of Apollo crowns the stern of the ship: and, as I said, this happened to have been done on the day before the trial. That was why Socrates lay so long in prison between his trial and his death.*

And what emotion filled the place! It was so powerful that it still breaks out in the narrator's feelings:

PHAEDO. *Well, I myself was strangely moved on that day. I did not feel that I was being present at the death of a dear friend: I did not pity him, for he seemed to me happy, Echecrates, both in his bearing and in his words, so fearlessly and nobly did he die. I could not help thinking that the gods would watch over him still on his journey to the other world, and that when he arrived there it would be well with him, if it was ever well with any man. Therefore I had scarcely any feeling of pity, as you would expect at such a mournful time. Neither did I feel the pleasure which I usually felt at our philosophical discussions,*[1] *for our talk was of philosophy. A very singular feeling came over me, a strange mixture of pleasure and of pain when I remembered that he was presently to die. All of us who were there were in much the same state, laughing and crying by turns; particularly Apollodorus. I think you know the man and his ways.*

The Opening Events

Echecrates asks who were present, and Phaedo gives a list of names. One feels how important is the sentence which interrupts it: "Plato, I believe, was ill." The speaker goes on:

On the previous days I and the others had always met in the morning at the court where the trial was held, which was close to the prison; and then we had gone in to Socrates. We used to wait each morning until the prison was opened, conversing: for it was not opened early. When it was opened we used to go in to Socrates, and we generally spent the whole day with him.

The account gives a glimpse of the time which elapsed between the condemnation and death of Socrates. Then Phaedo continues:

But on that morning we met earlier than usual; for the evening before we had learnt, on leaving the prison, that the ship had arrived from Delos. So we arranged to be at the usual place as early as possible. When we reached the prison the porter, who generally let us in, came out to us and bade us wait a little, and not to go in until he summoned us himself; "for the Eleven," he said, "are releasing

[1] The text puts it, very finely: "when we were in philosophy."

> *Socrates from his fetters, and giving directions for his death to-day." In no great while he returned and bade us enter.*

Socrates's wife with her little son has arrived before them:

> *So we went in and found Socrates just released, and Xanthippe —you know her—sitting by him, holding his child in her arms. When Xanthippe saw us, she wailed aloud, and cried, in her woman's way, "This is the last time, Socrates, that you will talk with your friends, or they with you." And Socrates glanced at Crito, and said, "Crito, let her be taken home." So some of Crito's servants led her away, weeping bitterly and beating her breast.*

The passage has a chilly air: the unregenerate heart of the ancients —or perhaps a miserly fate, not to be mastered even by a Socrates.

Then comes a minute trait, proving how well this master of perception knew how to attach profound reflections to any and every occurrence:

> *But Socrates sat up on the bed, and bent his leg and rubbed it with his hand, and while he was rubbing it said to us, How strange a thing is what men call pleasure! How wonderful is its relation to pain, which seems to be the opposite of it! They will not come to a man together: but if he pursues the one and gains it, he is almost forced to take the other also, as if they were two distinct things united at one end.*

The prisoner has been relieved of his fetters, and rubs his limbs, till now impeded; thus his words afforded a psychological observation apposite to the situation. If we look closer, however, the thought anticipates a later and more important one. For by representing pleasure and pain as absorbed in the entirety of life, he prepares the way for the relativizing of birth and death in respect of a total existence persisting through several incarnations.

Pleasure and pain are curious phenomena. They cannot exist together; when one comes, the other must go; and yet they are linked to one another. Aesop, Socrates thinks, would have made a fable out of it. The name does not come in by mere chance. Socrates has of late been occupied with him. For when Cebes, one of those present, hears the name mentioned, he says that Evenus, a mutual philosophical friend, has asked him to enquire the meaning of the report he has heard that Socrates has been composing poems in prison. Socrates replies:

> Then tell him the truth, Cebes, he said. Say that it was from no wish to pose as a rival to him, or to his poems. I knew that it would not be easy to do that. I was only testing the meaning of certain dreams, and acquitting my conscience about them, in case they should be bidding me make this kind of music.

He then relates the dream—a very strange one, which makes one think:

> The fact is this. The same dream often used to come to me in my past life, appearing in different forms at different times, but always saying the same words, "Socrates, work at music and compose it." Formerly I used to think that the dream was encouraging me and cheering me on in what was already the work of my life, just as the spectators cheer on different runners in a race. I supposed that the dream was encouraging me to create the music at which I was working already: for I thought that philosophy was the highest music, and my life was spent in philosophy. But then, after the trial, when the feast of the god delayed my death, it occurred to me that the dream might possibly be bidding me create music in the popular sense, and that in that case I ought to do so, and not to disobey.

And with a certain rationalistic parsimony—which is indeed part of his general character, but is promptly outweighed by the touching spontaneity of this obedience to the divine voice—Socrates tells how he has tried to fulfil the requirement. First he composed a hymn to Apollo; then he reflected that a poet should create, not from rational thought-processes, but from free imagination. Feeling, however, that he was not capable of that, he took over such "works of imagination" as he had at his disposal, namely some fables of Aesop. These he then put into verse, and so fulfilled the injunction of the dream as best he could.

★

THE MAIN DISCOURSE
(*Introductory*)

THE MESSAGE TO EVENUS
AND THE NATURE OF DEATH

THE GRAND motif then begins:

> *Tell Evenus this, Cebes, and bid him farewell from me; and tell him to follow me as quickly as he can, if he is wise. I, it seems, shall depart to-day, for that is the will of the Athenians.*
>
> *And Simmias said, What strange advice to give Evenus, Socrates! I have often met him, and from what I have seen of him, I think that he is certainly not at all the man to take it, if he can help it.*
>
> *What? he said, is not Evenus a philosopher?*
>
> *Yes, I suppose so, replied Simmias.*
>
> *Then Evenus will wish to die, he said, and so will every man who is worthy of having any part in this study. But he will not lay violent hands on himself; for that, they say, is wrong.*

The narrative continues, indicating by the outward gesture that the thought is becoming more serious:

> *And as he spoke he put his legs off the bed on to the ground, and remained sitting thus for the rest of the conversation.*
>
> *Then Cebes asked him, What do you mean, Socrates, by saying that it is wrong for a man to lay violent hands on himself, but that the philosopher will wish to follow the dying man?*
>
> *What, Cebes? Have you and Simmias been with Philolaus, and not heard about these things?*
>
> *Nothing very definite, Socrates.*
>
> *Well, I myself only speak of them from hearsay: yet there is no reason why I should not tell you what I have heard. Indeed, as I am setting out on a journey to the other world, what could be more fitting for me than to talk about my journey, and to consider what we imagine to be its nature? How could we better employ the interval between this and sunset?*

The condemned may not lawfully be executed till after sunset. Till then many hours have still to go. Most men would see in this time only the intolerable waiting for death as it approached ever nearer; he, however, will fill it in with philosophic discourse—and we may well understand from the foregoing pronouncement that Socrates held this last discourse with the same calmness and precision as all the countless others in houses and streets, gymnasium and workshops.

Cebes begins it with the question, why one may not take one's own life. Socrates replies that the proposition, "It is better to die than to live", is true "of all others alone absolutely and without exception";[1] it does not however mean suicide, but—as will presently be explained—the continual transition from the immediately vital and psychological to the spiritual.

> *The reason which the secret teaching gives, that man is in a kind of prison,[2] and that he may not set himself free, nor escape from it, seems to me rather profound and not easy to fathom. But I do think, Cebes, that it is true that the gods are our guardians, and that we men are a part of their property.*

Again it is emphasized:

> *Then in this way perhaps it is not unreasonable to hold that no man has a right to take his own life, but that he must wait until God sends some necessity upon him, as has now been sent upon me.*

Cebes, a sharp-witted young man, makes an objection: The "flock of the gods" is here on earth, here the gods are masters, and good masters too—why then should the philosopher be required to die and thus escape them? Socrates answers:

> *I should be wrong, Cebes and Simmias, he went on, not to grieve at death, if I did not think that I was going to live both with other gods who are good and wise, and with men who have died, and who*

---

[1] *Sic.* But the Greek should probably be rendered differently.—Tr.
[2] The word *phroura* is ambiguous: it means both actively watching and passively being watched and fenced round.

are better than the men of this world. But you must know that I hope that I am going to live among good men, though I am not quite sure of that. But I am as sure as I can be in such matters that I am going to live with gods who are very good masters. And therefore I am not so much grieved at death: I am confident that the dead have some kind of existence, and, as has been said of old, an existence that is far better for the good than for the wicked.

Simmias, the younger friend of Cebes, would like to know more:

Well, Socrates, said Simmias, do you mean to go away and keep this belief to yourself, or will you let us share it with you? It seems to me that we too have an interest in this good. And it will also serve as your defence, if you can convince us of what you say.

Here occurs another very brief interlude. It increases the tension; moreover, it places Socrates's character once more in a wonderfully intimate light.

I will try, he replied. But I think Crito has been wanting to speak to me. Let us first hear what he has to say.
Only, Socrates, said Crito, that the man who is going to give you the poison has been telling me to warn you not to talk much. He says that talking heats people, and that the action of the poison must not be counteracted by heat. Those who excite themselves sometimes have to drink it two or three times.
Let him be, said Socrates: let him mind his own business, and be prepared to give me the poison twice, or, if need be, thrice.
I knew that would be your answer, said Crito: but the man has been importunate.
Never mind him, he replied.

This is no Stoic gesture; the man is full of life. It is real superiority —and, to make it credible, the passionate interest of a great philosopher, who feels himself gripped by the problem and now puts everything else aside, even the question whether he is to die an easy or a hard death.

The Theme

But I wish now to explain to you, my judges, why it seems to me that a man who has really spent his life in philosophy has reason to be of good cheer when he is about to die, and may well hope after death to gain in the other world the greatest good. I will try to show you, Simmias and Cebes, how this may be.

The world, perhaps, does not see that those who rightly engage in philosophy, study only dying and death. And, if this be true, it would be surely strange for a man all through his life to desire only death, and then, when death comes to him, to be vexed at it, when it has been his study and his desire for so long.

Simmias has to laugh at these words, although he is "in no laughing mood". He thinks what people would say if they heard this. This supplies the background to the question, "in what sense true philosophers desire death and deserve death". But the discussion must take place among such as are existentially adapted to it: "We will speak of this among ourselves only, dismissing those people (who are not concerned in it)" (64c).

Death is separation from the body; being dead is the state in which "the soul, separated from the body, exists by itself". But the true philosopher detaches himself from the corporeal throughout his life, because of the very meaning of philosophizing. Whatever he may have to deal with and in every respect, he will "stand aloof from it, as far as he can, and turn towards the soul", and in this will "excel the rest of men". For—and here the thought touches the core of Platonic philosophy, namely the doctrine of reality and truth, true being and true knowledge—corporeal reality, to which sense-perception is co-ordinated, contains no genuine truth, but only a fluctuating content, apprehensible by uncertain opinion. Perception of real truth is only possible when the spiritual soul rises above sense-impressions. This will only be the case—will it not?—

when none of the senses, whether hearing, or sight, or pain, or pleasure, harasses her: when she has dismissed the body, and released herself as far as she can from all intercourse or contact with it, and so, coming to be as much alone with herself as is possible, strives after real truth.

That is so.

And here too the soul of the philosopher very greatly despises the body, and flies from it, and seeks to be alone by herself, does she not?

Clearly.

"That which is" is essential truth existing above phenomena; it is likewise the true and imperishable reality. This is made clear by an example:

And what do you say to the next point, Simmias? Do we say that there is such a thing as absolute justice, or not?

Indeed we do.

And absolute beauty, and absolute good?

Of course.

Have you ever seen any of them with your eyes?

Indeed, I have not, he replied.

Did you ever grasp them with any bodily sense? I am speaking of all absolutes, whether size, or health, or strength; in a word of the essence or real being of everything. Is the very truth of things contemplated by the body? Is it not rather the case that the man, who prepares himself most carefully to apprehend by his intellect the essence of each thing which he examines, will come nearest to the knowledge of it?

Certainly.

And will not a man attain to this pure thought most completely, if he goes to each thing, as far as he can, with his mind alone, taking neither sight, nor any other sense along with his reason in the process of thought, to be an encumbrance? In every case he will pursue pure and absolute being, with his pure intellect alone. He will be set free as far as possible from the eye, and the ear, and, in short, from the whole body, because intercourse with the body troubles the soul, and hinders her from gaining truth and wisdom. Is it not he who will attain the knowledge of real being, if any man will?

Cognition means for Plato something different from what will be formulated by his great disciple Aristotle. For the latter, things and their coherence make up reality; truth is the character of validity which is immanent in concrete being. The senses grasp individual things; the understanding works over the result of sense-perception, the ideas, extracts from them what is of universal validity, and expresses it in logical, abstract form, that is, in concepts. For Plato, however, truth is something at once valid and real. In fact it is the only real, self-subsistent, the Idea; while things represent mere half-realities. The senses, therefore, which are co-ordinate with things, grasp only half-truths, "opinions". If a man will possess himself of truth itself, his mind must free itself from all that is corporeal, even from his own senses, and turn itself with purely spiritual intuition to the Ideas.

This view of knowledge and the knower is not lightly to be dismissed. It is one of the four or five which have determined the history of philosophy. It is grand, bold and violent—in a certain sense, one can even say, inhuman; for it threatens to eliminate that sphere which in a special sense guarantees the human: the sphere of body and thing. Though again it is human in the very important sense that it is a man's prerogative alone to advance thus beyond all bounds of security, into danger and possible destruction—which is the result of these formulations. It is the man who stakes all on the spirit that appears here—and it is easy to understand that men who were still swathed in the protective bonds of organic existence, in instinct and symbol, could only feel this proclamation as a danger.

What follows discusses the various hindrances which arise from earthly life among things and events, and gives as the final choice: "either never to attain to knowledge, or only when we are dead; for then the soul will be by itself, separated from the body, but not till then" (66e–67a).

Hence the conclusion for the present hour:

And, my friend, said Socrates, if this be true, I have good hope that, when I reach the place whither I am going, I shall there, if anywhere, gain fully that which we have sought so earnestly in the past. And so I shall set forth cheerfully on the journey that is appointed me to-day, and so may every man who thinks that his mind is prepared and purified.

And once again:

In truth, then, Simmias, he said, the true philosopher studies to die, and to him of all men is death least terrible.

The thought is then taken up once more, and it is shown that in other cases too a man may freely resign himself to death—for example, through grief for a beloved one, or through bravery. But he does that not for the sake of death itself, for he considers death only as an evil. If he yet chooses it, he does so simply because it is the only way to avoid a greater evil—for instance, the loss of honour. He is brave, therefore, from fear. Real bravery would not spring from so contradictory a motive, but would choose death because it leads to the state of true life, that is, to the true relation to the Idea.

Thereupon the whole ends on a deeply religious note:

True virtue in reality is a kind of purifying from all these things: and temperance, and justice, and courage, and wisdom itself, are the purification. And I fancy that the men who established our mysteries had a very real meaning: in truth they have been telling us in parables all the time that whosoever comes to Hades uninitiated and profane, will lie in the mire; while he that has been purified and initiated shall dwell with the gods. For "the thyrsus-bearers are many", as they say in the mysteries, "but the inspired few." And by these last, I believe, are meant only the true philosophers. And I in my life have striven as hard as I was able, and have left nothing undone that I might become one of them. Whether I have striven in the right way, and whether I have succeeded or not, I suppose that I shall learn in a little while, when I reach the other world, if it be the will of God.

That is my defence, Simmias and Cebes, to show that I have reason for not being angry or grieved at leaving you and my masters here. I believe that in the next world, no less than in this, I shall meet with good masters and friends, though the multitude are incredulous of it. And if I have been more successful with you in my defence than I was with my Athenian judges, it is well.

Plato is neither the promulgator of an aesthetic life, nor the prophet of an idealistic contemplation. His conceptions are based on a specific experience, namely that of the reality of mind and of that to which mind is essentially referred, "that which is". Consequently mind is not abstract reason in the modern sense, but the real substance of man, the foundation of existence and the basic force of personal life. Its essential correlative is truth, the just and the beautiful, value and significance, the Idea; again, however, not in the modern sense of abstract validity, but understood in the manner indicated by the designation, as precise as it is impressive, "that which is": as the truly real; as the very self of value and reality, beside which empirical objects are as unreal as the body is beside the soul. It is only this experience that gives meaning to Plato's conceptions. The moment it fails, they can only appear eccentric and "idealistic". They are also based on a specific decision: the resolve to take that reciprocity of mind and Idea as the real and to build one's existence on it. Platonic thought is insofar serious as the thinker abandons the basis of bodily life and the sensuous phenomena correlated with it, and seeks by renunciation and training to enter the pure reciprocity of mind and Idea. Plato cannot be interpreted too unacademically. In his teaching one really hears the "call of death's boundary".

Perhaps this consideration throws a new light on Socrates's conduct before his judges. It may well be that an inmost "will to die" is at work in him, though of a different kind from that understood by Nietzsche. It would be the will to attain at last, by actual death, the freedom of the pure reciprocity of mind and Idea, after that "practice of death" which has accompanied his whole life as a philosopher. In the last resort, then, no longer anything ethical, not even the ethos of philosophical responsibility, but something metaphysical and religious, which bursts all bounds of "must" and "may"; a Dionysia of the spirit, as is hinted indeed in the words about the true thyrsus-bearers.

Thus the motifs are interwoven at the very beginning of the

dialogue. The impending death of Socrates appears as the expression of that dying which, according to Platonic conviction, lies in the very nature of philosophizing. Socrates is a philosopher not only in will and endeavour, but in being and destiny—thus his personality and his fate manifest what philosophy is. Therefore the conversations which follow will be speeches, not of consolation, but of revelation. In them comes to light the meaning of philosophy as existence. It ascertains the significance which justifies it, the reality on which it rests, and the power by which it exists.

This will for the spirit is anything rather than decadent. That it sometimes became so later—when the fundamental religious and ethical will slackened, and the aesthetic element gained the upper hand—is nothing to do with Plato. What he has to say implies no faint-heartedness, no incapacity for the building up of life, no dualistic hatred of things. For the same philosopher who as thinker strives upward to the world of pure spirit, returns as lawgiver and educator to the world of the body and of things. The "hatred" that prevails here is one that loves. This will for the spirit presupposes the body and things, in order by overcoming them to win other individuals; in fact one might almost say that it provides for the optimum of vigorous and beautiful forms of body and matter, so that this conquest may attain its fullest significance. Plato's spiritual will presupposes that plenary man of whom his educational theory speaks; and his demand for death can only be rightly understood by that intensity of life to which the *Republic* gives expression. As soon as this connection is loosened, Plato becomes "Platonism". This is certainly decadence; it also is a "falling-off" from the original conception itself.

When Socrates had finished, Cebes replied to him, and said, I think that for the most part you are right, Socrates. But men are very incredulous of what you have said of the soul. They fear that she will no longer exist anywhere when she has left the body, but that she will be destroyed and perish on the very day of death. They think that the moment that she is released and leaves the body, she will be dissolved and vanish away like breath or smoke, and thenceforward cease to exist at all. If she were to exist somewhere as a whole, released from the evils which you enumerated just now, we should have good reason to hope, Socrates, that what you say is true. But it will need no little persuasion and assurance to show that the soul exists after death, and continues to possess any power or wisdom.

Here the real problem of the dialogue is posed: that notion of philosophy and that picture of the true philosopher have a meaning only if there is something in man which outlasts the present life—the soul. And indeed this word means something different from the "strengthless shade" of the Homeric world. The latter could never support an existence like that with which Plato is concerned. It is a depotentialized man, lacking the density of body, the warmth of blood, the light of consciousness, the power of volition and the fulness of perception; conceived after the manner of the shadow thrown by an object or of the shape that appears in a dream. The soul, however, that Plato has in mind is absolute reality, higher than everything the lack of which constitutes a "shade"; capable, therefore, of surviving the loss of life; indeed so fashioned that it is only through this that it attains the full freedom of its nature. Just as little is Plato's soul to be confused with the departed spirit of primitive religion. This is a real being, but belongs to a region which is foreign to and contrasted with the life of this present world; it is a being not to be comprehended from this side, differently orientated, and arousing terror. It is full of energy; but of a fearful kind, destructive of earthly life; an energy that can only be held off by anxious awe, manifold sacrifice and painstaking religious and magical precautions. The soul, however, that Plato has in mind is orientated to the light, capable of realizing every kind and degree of the good. It looks beyond the present life and is destined to transcend it; but in such a way that it takes with it the significant content of the latter, indeed only then truly realizes it. Its cognate sphere is above, and its proper movement an ascent. It is a question therefore of the discovery of the spirit—that spirit which is determined by truth and goodness, and is the subject of valid action, and thereby not only is real, but is ultimately the only real. The discovery of the spiritual soul is bound up with that of self-subsistent truth and impossible without this.

Is all this fact? Is man's soul such that he can die confident that the essential part of him will remain alive and fulfil the meaning of his existence?

> *True, Cebes, said Socrates; but what are we to do? Do you wish to converse about these matters and see if what I say is probable?*
>
> *I for one, said Cebes, should gladly hear your opinion about them.*
>
> *I think, said Socrates, that no one who heard me now, even if he were a comic poet, would say that I am an idle talker about things which do not concern me. So, if you wish it, let us examine this question.*
>
> *Let us consider whether or no the souls of men exist in the next world after death, thus.*

THE MAIN DISCOURSE
(First Part)

THE RELATIVITY OF BIRTH AND DEATH

"LET US consider whether or no the souls of men exist in the next world after death," begins the discussion. And it at once takes a peculiar turn, in that the soul's capacity for outlasting the perishable earthly life is expressed by an obviously Orphic saying:

> *There is an ancient belief, which we remember, that on leaving this world they exist there, and that they return hither and are born again from the dead. But if it be true that the living are born from the dead, our souls must exist in the other world: otherwise they could not be born again.*

If birth means that a soul passes from the sphere of death, or more accurately, from the state of being dead, being on the other side, into the state of earthly life, it must have existed there already. In that case, however, the future death of the being which now begins to live cannot mean that it is annihilated, but only that its soul returns to the state of "being dead" which it was in before its birth. This argument conceives existence as a whole which realizes itself in a transition through different spheres, here and hereafter, and in a succession of different states, a transcendental and an earthly form of existence. Being born and dying are then the respective passages from the one sphere and state to the other, and point back to a third, underlying reality which persists through them—that is to say that, taken separately, they have no independent and self-intelligible character, but only a dialectical one.

This is at once explained more fully:

Well, said he, the easiest way of answering the question will be to consider it not in relation to men only, but also in relation to all animals and plants, and in short to all things that are generated. Is it the case that everything, which has an opposite, is generated only from its opposite?

Then comes a series of examples: The greater arises from the lesser, the lesser from the greater, the stronger from the weaker, the faster from the slower, the worse from the better, the more just from the less just, the separate from the mixed, the warmer from the cooler, etc. The sense of the examples is clear: states are mentioned which have indeed a different character—"opposite" according to the loosely used word—but are referred to an identical standard and an identical underlying reality. Although, then, they are mutually "opposite" and exclude one another, they yet arise "from one another".

The pretended character of the relations mentioned is, however, only apparent; in reality it is merely a question of differences of degree. Not so the following passage, which is genuinely dialectical in construction and leads with suggestive force to the goal of the discussion, namely the relation of sleeping and waking with its respective transitions:

Now, said Socrates, I will explain to you one of the two pairs of opposites of which I spoke just now, and its generations, and you shall explain to me the other. Sleep is the opposite of waking. From sleep is produced the state of waking: and from the state of waking is produced sleep. Their generations are, first, to fall asleep; secondly, to awake.

Cebes must think further according to this scheme:

Now then, said he, do you tell me about life and death. Death is the opposite of life, is it not?
It is.
And they are generated the one from the other?
Yes.
Then what is that which is generated from the living?
The dead, he replied.
And what is generated from the dead?
I must admit that it is the living.
Then living things and living men are generated from the dead, Cebes?
Clearly, said he.
Then our souls exist in the other world? he said.
Apparently.

The other side of the relation is now considered:

Now of these two generations the one is certain? Death I suppose is certain enough, is it not?
Yes, quite, he replied.
What then shall we do? said he. Shall we not assign an opposite generation to correspond? Or is nature imperfect here? Must we not assign some opposite generation to dying?
I think so, certainly, he said.
And what must it be?
To come to life again.
And if there be such a thing as a return to life, he said, it will be a generation from the dead to the living, will it not?
It will, certainly.

Finally, the result of the whole:

Then we are agreed on this point: namely, that the living are generated from the dead no less than the dead from the living. But we agreed that, if this be so, it is a sufficient proof that the souls of the dead must exist somewhere, whence they come into being again.

What follows confirms this by an explanation: If there were a change, a "becoming", only in one direction, from life to death, and not also in the reverse direction, from death to life, then "all life would finally be swallowed up in death". The movement of becoming, then, must be in both directions: which supposes that the soul already existed before birth and will still exist after death.

Accurately considered, what happens is not that the "greater" arises from the "lesser", but that the same thing has first a lesser and then a greater dimension. Both dimensions are determinations of the same thing and are connected with one another by the process of extension. In the same way, "sleeping" does not arise from "waking", but the same being is first awake and then asleep, and remains the same throughout these different states of life. More weighty is the further objection that the whole train of thought rests on a mythical or metaphysical presupposition. According to this there is in life a content which remains eternally the same, and which must ever be compensated anew on the one side for what it loses on the other: an assumption which has been taken over more or less consciously from the doctrine of reincarnation. But what the argument really means is this: being dead, or to speak more accurately, being without body, constitutes a state; being alive, or more accurately, being embodied, likewise. Existence passes through both states in turn, throughout the "becoming" of our life. Entrance into the first is dying, into the second, being born. There must be something underlying and supporting the whole: namely the soul, which, existing before birth, entered the realm of incorporeal being by a previous death.

That being alive and being dead, being born and dying actually stand in this dialectical relation to one another, is not proved. Strictly speaking, nothing whatever is proved here, but only an experience expressed—that of an ultimate core of existence, lying behind the particular life-phenomena. It must not be confused with the Dionysiac experience. In this too, birth and death are made relative to something essential, namely the whole of life. By birth the shape of the individual being is formed from the total stream, by death it is again resolved into it: a transitory wave in that stream of life which realizes itself through all becoming and decay. To formulate this differently: in dying the individual form breaks up. This, however, means not only that something significant disintegrates, but also that something which was a limit and a fetter is burst open by the force of the totality of life. Herein death, the apparent destruction of life, shows itself as the culmination of life's totality triumphing over every particular form—the counterpart of birth, in which the totality is likewise active, but in order to allow, by the act of self-restriction, the emergence of the separate form. In both processes the present life is the ultimate and essential thing to which all separate phenomena are made relative. The individual form seems to be independent within the bounds of birth and death; actually, however, it is the whole running through the individual life-spans which is real, so that for this experience there is no more a true death, in the sense of a real ending, than there is a true birth, in the sense of a real beginning.

At first sight it would seem as though Socrates's arguments represented this line of thought, which—with more or less variation—sways all mythical and Dionysiac speculation, to continue its career later in the various forms of metaphysical or biological monism. But what Plato means is something radically different. The real thing to which he makes life and death relative, is not the vital whole streaming through time, but the self-based core of individual existence. The limitation of its span is overcome, not by taking it as a vanishing quantity compared with the vastness of the whole, but by having recourse to something which is qualitatively different both from the individual's life-history, with its beginning and end, and from the total stream of life in general: namely the mind. Man experiences himself as a mind, and perceives that beginning and end of the earthly lifetime have for such no absolute significance, but are subordinate to the individual sense of existence which the mind supports. The Dionysiac experience of victory feels individual existence to be immaterial, and throws itself into the great coherence of life as into the real; the Platonic experience, on the contrary, discovers the real precisely in the spiritual core of individual existence and nullifies by its indestructibility the beginning and ending processes of her present life.

The fact that the doctrine of reincarnation emerges in this context, shows the religious nature of the whole interpretation of existence. Apart from its metaphysical assertions, it expresses a definite and fundamental consciousness, according to which the reality of existence is not enclosed by birth and death, but extends far beyond them into the supratemporal and supramundane and makes the temporal relative. The temporal appears as a transitional stage: man comes from elsewhere and goes elsewhere. All this gives to the mind, and through it to man, a certain strangeness and mystery; and it is this which, together with the luminous actuality of the Greek nature, gives its peculiar character to the Platonic conception of existence.

Logically as well as materially there is much to object to in the argument, but what Plato is really concerned about is to counteract the overwhelming impression made by the process of death, and not of death in general, but of that which the speaker Socrates must himself soon undergo. This dying process becomes something immaterial, just as that process which took place once at the beginning of his life—being born—was immaterial. This is not only thought and said, but carried out with the deepest sincerity. The intrinsic force of the living spirit drives through the man's own perishableness to something lasting, which is beyond all change and has nothing to do either with being born or with dying. As long as one merely examines the arguments formally or materially, they look like a semi-logical play with half-meanings; they reveal their true meaning only when one penetrates to what really matters: how this man, ready for death and so intensely alive, evokes from himself the innermost thing in him, the consciousness of his spiritual soul; how this is distinguished from all that is contained in the biological flux, in the sphere of birth and death, and therein assures itself of its imperishability.

This, of course, brings to mind two special and complementary dangers of Platonic thought. The first of these is the nullifying of the historical. If birth and death are processes alien to the soul's nature, affecting only its garment, its house, nay its prison, earthly life as such loses its seriousness. The spirit, the person, have no binding habitation in it, but merely pass through it. The existential density of man is dissolved—of man, who not only has but is a body;

who is not an eternal being sojourning for a while in a temporal order which is foreign to it; but as a spiritual being exists historically, that is, in time, and whose temporal behaviour decides an eternal life. The spirit is superior to the body and more real; but time attaches to the body; and history depends on the fact that the spirit exists in the body, as man. The danger of effacing the historical process appears also, therefore, in the proposition that the individual life repeats itself. For, if that happens, the value of the person in the flesh, the decision fraught with eternity in time, the seriousness, the splendour and the tragedy of the unique occurrence, disappear. The doctrine of reincarnation abolishes history. The other danger is the counterpart of the first: "spirit" is made equivalent to "eternal being". As the consciousness that death does not touch the soul's essence is exaggerated into the assertion that it does not enter into the range of the existentially serious at all, but is something external, so also the consciousness that the spiritual soul is indestructible is exaggerated into the assertion that it is uncreated, eternal. The spiritual experience in question here is so powerful that it breaks through its bounds and confuses the essentially different categories of indestructibility and uncreatedness: a spiritual Dionysism, so to speak, which betrays itself by its mythological background. It too throws into doubt the seriousness of human life, the sobriety of the real soul, the truth of the real human spirit, which is certainly indestructible, but not uncreated, certainly a genuine spirit, but not God.

The Argument Confirmed: Anamnêsis

Cebes now supports this reference of the present life back to a previous one with a new argument:

And besides, Socrates, rejoined Cebes, if the doctrine which you are fond of stating, that our learning is only a process of recollection, be true, then I suppose we must have learnt at some former time what we recollect now. And that would be impossible unless our souls had existed somewhere before they came into this human form. So that is another reason for believing the soul immortal.

His young friend Simmias has not quite grasped the argument:

But, Cebes, interrupted Simmias, what are the proofs of that? Recall them to me: I am not very clear about them at present.

One argument, answered Cebes, and the strongest of all, is that if you question men about anything in the right way, they will answer you correctly of themselves. But they would not have been able to do that, unless they had had within themselves knowledge and right reason. Again, show them such things as geometrical diagrams, and the proof of the doctrine is complete.

The whole life of the Socratic-Platonic circle comes into view in this passage: the asking of questions "in the right way", that great art of Socrates; the wonderful experience of how in this questioning something stirs in the mind of the one questioned, something that had remained to him strange hitherto, namely the knowledge of essence together with the place which it inhabits—so utterly different from empirical thinking and its sphere—absolute and eternal, and yet recognized as most intimately one's own. One feels the overwhelming experience from which the critical philosophy arose, the experience of valid knowledge, which becomes aware of its own peculiarity and wonders where it comes from, since it cannot possibly come out of the empirical. The Platonic answer is: It comes from an existence which lies before birth. As soon as it takes place, then, reminiscence takes place.

Socrates notices that Simmias does not yet feel happy about it:

And if that does not convince you, Simmias, said Socrates, look at the matter in another way and see if you agree then. You have doubts, I know, how what is called knowledge can be recollection.

Nay, replied Simmias, I do not doubt. But I want to recollect the argument about recollection. What Cebes undertook to explain has nearly brought your theory back to me and convinced me. But I am none the less ready to hear how you undertake to explain it.

In this way, he returned.

Thereupon the Master expounds the doctrine of *anamnêsis* thoroughly. First he speaks about "being reminded" in general:

The knowledge of a man is different from the knowledge of a lyre, is it not?

Certainly.

And you know that when lovers see a lyre, or a garment, or anything that their favourites are wont to use, they have this feeling. They know the lyre, and in their mind they receive the image of the youth whose the lyre was. That is recollection. For instance, someone seeing Simmias often is reminded of Cebes; and there are endless examples of the same thing.

Indeed there are, said Simmias.

Is not that a kind of recollection, he said; and more especially when a man has this feeling with reference to things which the lapse of time and inattention have made him forget?

Yes, certainly, he replied.

This reminiscence may arise either from the relation of likeness—for example, between the painted picture of a man and the man himself—or from that of unlikeness—say rather, of some contrast. At the same time the person who remembers forms a judgment as to how far the likeness or unlikeness goes. This judgment can only rest on the fact that he has in his consciousness "the equal itself", the phenomenon of equality as such—and also, be it added, "the unequal itself", the phenomenon of unrelatedness. By these he measures the different empirical relations of equality or inequality which he meets with. Now these relations never realize equality or inequality perfectly, but only approximately; therefore knowledge about the phenomenon itself cannot be derived from experience:

At any rate it is by the senses that we must perceive that all sensible objects strive to resemble absolute equality, and are inferior to it. Is not that so?

Yes.

Then before we began to see, and to hear, and to use the other senses, we must have received the knowledge of the nature of abstract and real equality; otherwise we could not have compared equal sensible objects with abstract equality, and seen that the former in all cases strive to be like the latter, though they are always inferior to it?

That is the necessary consequence of what we have been saying, Socrates.

Hence the inference:

Did we not see, and hear, and possess the other senses as soon as we were born?

Yes, certainly.

And we must have received the knowledge of abstract equality before we had these senses?

Yes.

Then, it seems, we must have received that knowledge before we were born?

It does.

It is the doctrine of the Idea, which answers the question as to the cause of valid knowledge. True knowing is accordingly knowing in the light of the absolute forms of being. These cannot be obtained from things, because nothing perceptible by the senses adequately represents its essential form. Therefore they must be found in themselves, in a sphere which is raised above every defect. To the question how the mind gets there, the Platonic dialogues have two answers. According to the one, when the mind, exalted by love, frees itself from the sensible aspects of a thing, it beholds that thing's essential form, the Idea. The other answer is that the mind has once, while it was yet unborn and free from the body, beheld the Idea, and then through birth forgotten it; but as soon as it concentrates itself on the phenomenon in genuine thought, it remembers the Idea. The "beyond", the distinction between the mental-categorical and the sensuous-contingent, is expressed in the first answer in a psychologically metaphysical way, by an asceticism, if one may call it so, of the act of cognition; in the second answer it is expressed in a biographically metaphysical way, by a mythology of antenatal existence. In both cases valid knowledge is conjoined with death: in the first case as the sphere, detached from the present partnership of body and soul, of the purely spiritual act; in the second case as the sphere, separated from earthly life, of purely spiritual existence.

Now if we received this knowledge before our birth, and were born with it, we knew, both before, and at the moment of our birth, not only the equal, and the greater, and the less, but also everything of the same kind, did we not? Our present reasoning does not refer only to equality. It refers just as much to absolute good, and absolute beauty, and absolute justice, and absolute holiness; in short, I repeat, to everything which we mark with the name of the real, in the questions and answers of our dialectic. So we must have received our knowledge of all realities before we were born.

That is so.

And we must always be born with this knowledge, and must always retain it throughout life, if we have not each time forgotten it, after having received it. For to know means to receive and retain knowledge, and not to have lost it. Do not we mean by forgetting the loss of knowledge, Simmias?

Yes, certainly, Socrates, he said.

But, I suppose, if it be the case that we lost at birth the knowledge which we received before we were born, and then afterwards, by using our senses on the objects of sense, recovered the knowledge which we had previously possessed, then what we call learning is the recovering of knowledge which is already ours. And are we not right in calling that recollection?

Certainly.

Hence now the inference, quite *ad hominem:*

Then which do you choose, Simmias? Are we born with knowledge, or do we recollect the things of which we have received knowledge before our birth?

I cannot say at present, Socrates.

Well, have you an opinion about this question? Can a man who knows give an account of what he knows, or not? What do you think about that?

Yes, of course he can, Socrates.

And do you think that every one can give an account of the ideas of which we have been speaking?

I wish I did, indeed, said Simmias: but I am very much afraid that by this time to-morrow there will no longer be any man living able to do so as it should be done.

> *Then, Simmias, he said, you do not think that all men know these things?*
>
> *Certainly not.*
>
> *Then they recollect what they once learned?*
>
> *Necessarily.*
>
> *And when did our souls gain this knowledge? It cannot have been after we were born men.*
>
> *No, certainly not.*
>
> *Then it was before?*
>
> *Yes.*
>
> *Then, Simmias, our souls existed formerly, apart from our bodies, and possessed intelligence before they came into man's shape.*
>
> *Unless we receive this knowledge at the moment of birth, Socrates. That time still remains.*
>
> *Well, my friend: and at what other time do we lose it? We agreed just now that we are not born with it: do we lose it at the same moment that we gain it? or can you suggest any other time?*
>
> *I cannot, Socrates. I did not see that I was talking nonsense.*

And then the final result:

> *Then, Simmias, he said, is not this the truth? If, as we are for ever repeating, beauty, and good, and the other ideas really exist, and if we refer all the objects of sensible perception to these ideas which were formerly ours, and which we find to be ours still, and compare sensible objects with them, then, just as they exist, our souls must have existed before ever we were born. But if they do not exist, then our reasoning will have been thrown away. Is it so? If these ideas exist, does it not at once follow that our souls must have existed before we were born, and if they do not exist, then neither did our souls?*
>
> *Admirably put, Socrates, said Simmias. I think that the necessity is the same for the one as for the other. The reasoning has reached a place of safety in the common proof of the existence of our souls before we were born, and of the existence of the ideas of which you spoke. Nothing is so evident to me as that beauty, and good, and the other ideas, which you spoke of just now, have a very real existence indeed. Your proof is quite sufficient for me.*

These arguments contain some significant sentences: "If, as we are for ever repeating, beauty, and good, and the other ideas really exist . . . then, just as they exist, our souls must have existed before ever we were born. . . ." Here is a conception which goes beyond the mere statement of pre-existence. According to this notion the Idea exists necessarily, and with the same necessity the soul also. This means that the soul is of the genus of the Idea. An important conception, which will be taken up again later.

THE MAIN DISCOURSE

(A Doubt, and First Interlude)

SIMMIAS is satisfied.

> *But what of Cebes? said Socrates. I must convince Cebes too.*
> *I think that he is satisfied, said Simmias, though he is the most sceptical of men in argument. But I think that he is perfectly convinced that our souls existed before we were born.*
> *But I do not think myself, Socrates, he continued, that you have proved that the soul will continue to exist when we are dead. The common fear which Cebes spoke of, that she may be scattered to the winds at death, and that death may be the end of her existence, still stands in the way. Assuming that the soul is generated and comes together from some other elements, and exists before she ever enters the human body, why should she not come to an end and be destroyed, after she has entered into the body, when she is released from it?*
> *You are right, Simmias, said Cebes. I think that only half the required proof has been given. It has been shown that our souls existed before we were born; but it must also be shown that our souls will continue to exist after we are dead, no less than that they existed before we were born, if the proof is to be complete.*

Socrates indeed thinks that with the proof of the soul's pre-existence its survival also beyond death is confirmed. For as soon as one has recourse to the argument of the relativity of birth and death, the following conclusion results: If earthly life originates from the state of death, or more accurately, from the incorporeal existence of the other world, then conversely, from the death of the body must arise a new existence of bodiless spirituality. Then follows the fine passage:

> Still I think that you and Simmias would be glad to discuss this question further. Like children, you are afraid that the wind will really blow the soul away and disperse her when she leaves the body; especially if a man happens to die in a storm and not in a calm.
>
> Cebes laughed and said, Try and convince us as if we were afraid, Socrates; or rather, do not think that we are afraid ourselves. Perhaps there is a child within us who has these fears. Let us try and persuade him not to be afraid of death, as if it were a bugbear.
>
> You must charm him every day, until you have charmed him away, said Socrates.
>
> And where shall we find a good charmer, Socrates, he asked, now that you are leaving us?
>
> Hellas is a large country, Cebes, he replied, and good men may doubtless be found in it; and the nations of the Barbarians are many. You must search them all through for such a charmer, sparing neither money nor labour; for there is nothing on which you could spend money more profitably. And you must search for him among yourselves too, for you will hardly find a better charmer than yourselves.
>
> That shall be done, said Cebes. But let us return to the point where we left off, if you will.
>
> Yes, I will: why not?
>
> Very good, he replied.

THE MAIN DISCOURSE
(Second Part)

INDESTRUCTIBILITY OF THE SOUL

So SOCRATES formulates the problem thus:

> Well, said Socrates, must we not ask ourselves this question? What kind of thing is liable to suffer dispersion, and for what kind of thing have we to fear dispersion? And then we must see whether the

soul belongs to that kind or not, and be confident or afraid about our own souls accordingly.

Only what is composite can be decomposed. Composition and decomposition represent the same process, but in contrary directions. That being would be uncompounded which "always remains in the same state and unchanging". But that which is "always changing and never the same is most likely to be compounded". Mutability in time denotes composition, constancy in time simplicity of nature.

Here emerges one of the fundamental axioms of the Platonic view of being and the world: The nobler, the simpler. "Simplicity" however does not mean poverty of content or primitiveness, but the contrary of these: fulness of content, richness of value and being— but in the form of comprehension. To this corresponds the other principle: The nobler, the more constant. Again however immutability does not mean rigidity. The criticism that the Platonic view of being is static proceeds from a special conception of movement. Whenever act, life and fecundity are seen only in the alternation of actions and states, this primacy of simplicity and immutability certainly implies stiffness. But these Platonic axioms proceed from a different fundamental experience, according to which there is not only the transitory act which a subject directs towards an object, and which begins, completes itself and ends—but also the immanent act, which goes on in the agent itself and tends towards a state. The former is of its nature transient; the more real it is, the more clearly it has beginning, progress and end. The latter however aims at duration. Its form is inner mobility, vibration. It would be perfect if it coincided with being itself. Even then there would be activity and life, but as self-collected vigilance, actuality, tension and rest simultaneously.[1] This conception of life is connected also with the idea of simplicity. That mode of existence is perfect in which fulness of content goes with simplicity of the totally collected and transparent form, and act and vitality are realized in pure compenetration and development of its own essence. This complex

---

[1] Compare, for example, Boethius's notion of eternity: "Eternity is the comprehensive and perfect possession of infinite life" (*De cons. phil.*, V, 6).

of ideas is rooted in contemplation, in the experience of a life unfolding itself upward and inwardly by quiet and concentration.

From this standpoint the force of the Platonic arguments becomes clearer:

> *Does the being, which in our dialectic we define as meaning absolute existence, remain always in exactly the same state, or does it change? Do absolute equality, absolute beauty, and every other absolute existence, admit of any change at all? or does absolute existence in each case, being essentially uniform, remain the same and unchanging, and never in any case admit of any sort or kind of change whatsoever?*

If the above-mentioned axioms are true of anything, they are true of that which signifies the fulness of being simply: the Idea. For it is this which makes possible the statements "this is this" and "this means that", which form the nucleus of knowledge. It is thus absolutely univocal, free from anything extraneous; entirely and exclusively coincident with itself, therefore at once full and simple, real and immutable.

Not so the manifold reality of things, which is formed after that original pattern:

> *And what of the many beautiful things, such as men, and horses, and garments, and the like, and of all which bears the names of the ideas, whether equal, or beautiful, or anything else? Do they remain the same, or is it exactly the opposite with them? In short, do they never remain the same at all, either in themselves or in their relations?*
>
> *These things, said Cebes, never remain the same.*

To these two spheres correspond different acts of perception in man:

> *You can touch them, and see them, and perceive them with the other senses, while you can grasp the unchanging only by the reasoning of the intellect. These latter are invisible and not seen. Is it not so?*
>
> *That is perfectly true, he said.*

The movement of the thought is clear: Things are manifold, composite, therefore perishable; the Ideas are uncompounded, simple, therefore indestructible. The action of the senses is directed towards things, and so shares their nature; the act of purely intellectual cognition is directed towards the Ideas, and so shares the nature of Ideas.

> *Let us assume then, he said, if you will, that there are two kinds of existence, the one visible, the other invisible.*
> *Yes, he said.*
> *And the invisible is unchanging, while the visible is always changing.*
> *Yes, he said again.*
> *Are not we men made up of body and soul?*
> *There is nothing else, he replied.*
> *And which of these kinds of existence should we say that the body is most like, and most akin to?*
> *The visible, he replied; that is quite obvious.*
> *And the soul? Is that visible or invisible?*
> *It is invisible to man, Socrates, he said.*
> *But we mean by visible and invisible, visible and invisible to man; do we not?*
> *Yes; that is what we mean.*
> *Then what do we say of the soul? Is it visible, or not visible?*
> *It is not visible.*
> *Then is it invisible?*
> *Yes.*
> *Then the soul is more like the invisible than the body; and the body is like the visible.*
> *That is necessarily so, Socrates.*

All this means that the nature of the soul—and here the thought touched on above is followed out to the end—is similar to that towards which its essential act, namely pure knowledge, is directed. The soul is itself simple and indestructible.

In the next passage the same thing is explained again and more emphatically.

> *Have we not also said[1] that, when the soul employs the body in any inquiry, and makes use of sight, or hearing, or any other sense,—*

[1] 65b, not translated here.

for inquiry with the body means inquiry with the senses,—she is dragged away by it to the things which never remain the same, and wanders about blindly, and becomes confused and dizzy, like a drunken man, from dealing with things that are ever changing?

Certainly.

But when she investigates any question by herself, she goes away to the pure, and eternal, and immortal, and unchangeable, to which she is akin, and so she comes to be ever with it, as soon as she is by herself, and can be so: and then she rests from her wanderings, and dwells with it unchangingly, for she is dealing with what is unchanging? And is not this state of the soul called wisdom?[1]

Indeed, Socrates, you speak well and truly, he replied.

Which kind of existence do you think from our former and our present arguments that the soul is more like and more akin to?

I think, Socrates, he replied, that after this inquiry the very dullest man would agree that the soul is infinitely more like the unchangeable than the changeable.

And the body?

That is like the changeable.

There are certain primitive forms of philosophical experience; the one in question here declares truth to be the basis of being. This does not mean that truth is in the service of being—any sort of pragmatism would be fatal to what is meant—but that reality depends ultimately on validity; that a being is to that extent real to which it affirms and accomplishes a truth which is wholly disinterested, purely self-subsistent and valid for its own sake. Thus truth—the Idea—is that which simply is. But the mind is co-ordinated to the Idea, and so participates in its state of being. Firstly in virtue of its nature, simply because it is mind—that primary essence which in the evolution of life becomes more and more differentiated from the material. Secondly on the ground of its

---

[1] *Phronêsis*: the word is richer in meaning than the ethically stressed "prudence". It signifies the full development of understanding, a living in knowledge, an existing in intercourse with the truth.

tendency, in that a man's mind becomes the more real the more exclusively he attends to the Idea.

It is this experience which is the underlying motive of the *Phaedo*, and which its arguments seek to elucidate.

These latter are not abstractly correct "proofs", even though they claim to be such in the first instance. In fact they do nothing more than interpret that awareness in logical terms.

> *Now tell me, Cebes; is the result of all we have said that the soul is most like the divine, and the immortal, and the intelligible, and the uniform, and the indissoluble, and the unchangeable; while the body is most like the human, and the mortal, and the unintelligible, and the multiform, and the dissoluble, and the changeable?*

The Philosophic Way of Life

The investigation ends with some religious and practical reflections. A dead body decomposes more or less rapidly; if it is embalmed, it may even last a very long time. But it is different with the soul. It has the possibility and the duty of going

> *hence to a place that is like herself, glorious, and pure, and invisible, to Hades, which is rightly called the unseen world, to dwell with the good and wise God, whither, if it be the will of God, my soul too must shortly go.*

This is the goal for which she must prepare herself, thus:

> *I will tell you what happens to a soul which is pure at her departure, and which in her life has had no intercourse that she could avoid with the body, and so draws after her, when she dies, no taint of the body, but has shunned it, and gathered herself into herself, for such has been her constant study;—and that only means that she has loved wisdom rightly, and has truly practised how to die. Is not this the practice of death?*

If she does this,

does not the soul, then, which is in that state, go away to the invisible that is like herself, and to the divine, and the immortal, and the wise, where she is released from error, and folly, and fear, and fierce passions, and all the other evils that fall to the lot of men, and is happy, and for the rest of time lives in very truth with the gods, as they say that the initiated do? Shall we affirm this, Cebes?

Yes, certainly, said Cebes.

But if she refuses to do this, and

if she be defiled and impure when she leaves the body, from being ever with it, and serving it, and loving it, and from being besotted by it, and by its desires and pleasures, so that she thinks nothing true, but what is bodily, and can be touched, and seen, and eaten, and drunk, and used for men's lusts; if she has learnt to hate, and tremble at, and fly from what is dark and invisible to the eye, and intelligible and apprehended by philosophy—do you think that a soul which is in that state will be pure and without alloy at her departure?

No, indeed, he replied.

She is penetrated, I suppose, by the corporeal, which the unceasing intercourse and company and care of the body has made a part of her nature.

Yes.

Her existence will then be a corresponding one:

And, my dear friend, the corporeal must be burdensome, and heavy and earthy, and visible; and it is by this that such a soul is weighed down and dragged back to the visible world, because she is afraid of the invisible world of Hades, and haunts, it is said, the graves and tombs, where shadowy forms of souls have been seen, which are the phantoms of souls which were impure at their release, and still cling to the visible; which is the reason why they are seen.

That is likely enough, Socrates.

That is likely, certainly, Cebes: and these are not the souls of the good, but of the evil, which are compelled to wander in such places as a punishment for the wicked lives that they have lived.

As these souls are entirely bound to the corporeal, they must soon enter into bodies again—and into such, of course, as are similar to their inferior nature, that is, into animal bodies—and those of such animals as have most affinity with their respective characters.

This consideration makes it imperative to lead a philosophic life:

None but the philosopher or the lover of knowledge, who is wholly pure when he goes hence, is permitted to go to the race of the gods.

And again:

The lovers of knowledge know that when philosophy receives the soul, she is fast bound in the body, and fastened to it: she is unable to contemplate what is, by herself, or except through the bars of her prison-house, the body; and she is wallowing in utter ignorance. And philosophy sees that the dreadful thing about the imprisonment is that it is caused by lust, and that the captive herself is an accomplice in her own captivity. The lovers of knowledge, I repeat, know that philosophy takes the soul when she is in this condition, and gently encourages her, and strives to release her from her captivity, showing her that the perceptions of the eye, and the ear, and the other senses, are full of deceit, and persuading her to stand aloof from the senses, and to use them only when she must, and exhorting her to rally and gather herself together, and to trust only to herself, and to the real existence which she of her own self apprehends: and to believe that nothing which is subject to change, and which she perceives by other faculties, has any truth, for such things are visible and sensible, while what she herself sees is apprehended by reason and invisible. The soul of the true philosopher thinks that it would be wrong to resist this deliverance from captivity, and therefore she holds aloof, so far as she can, from pleasure, and desire, and pain, and fear; for she reckons that when a man has vehement pleasure, or fear, or pain, or desire, he suffers from them, not merely the evils which might be expected, such as sickness, or some loss arising from the indulgence of his desires; he suffers what is the greatest and last of evils, and does not take it into account.

What do you mean, Socrates? asked Cebes.

> I mean that when the soul of any man feels vehement pleasure or pain, she is forced at the same time to think that the object, whatever it be, of these sensations is the most distinct and truest, when it is not. Such objects are chiefly visible ones, are they not?
>
> They are.
>
> And is it not in this state that the soul is most completely in bondage to the body?
>
> How so?
>
> Because every pleasure and pain has a kind of nail, and nails and pins her to the body, and gives her a bodily nature, making her think that whatever the body says is true. And so, from having the same fancies and the same pleasures as the body, she is obliged, I suppose, to come to have the same ways, and way of life: she must always be defiled with the body when she leaves it, and cannot be pure when she reaches the other world; and so she soon falls back into another body, and takes root in it, like seed that is sown. Therefore she loses all part in intercourse with the divine, and pure, and uniform.

This, then, is the Master's last answer to the questions of the two young men:

> The soul of a philosopher will consider that it is the office of philosophy to set her free. She will know that she must not give herself up once more to the bondage of pleasure and pain, from which philosophy is releasing her, and, like Penelope, do a work, only to undo it continually, weaving instead of unweaving her web. She gains for herself peace from these things, and follows reason and ever abides in it, contemplating what is true and divine and real, and fostered up by them. So she thinks that she should live in this life, and when she dies she believes that she will go to what is akin to and like herself, and be released from human ills. A soul, Simmias and Cebes, that has been so nurtured, and so trained, will never fear lest she should be torn in pieces at her departure from the body, and blown away by the winds, and vanish, and utterly cease to exist.

The answer to Evenus has now been justified. It has become clear how seriously it was meant and how much of a piece it was with the inmost purpose of Platonic philosophy.

This is not the place to examine the thesis itself—to ask whether the act of thinking really represents a purely spiritual act, and whether human and philosophical existence should be founded on it; or whether on the contrary every act, even that which is distinguished by the highest value in the scale, is human, that is, at once spiritual and corporeal. Plato at least maintains that true thinking is of a purely spiritual nature and directed towards a similar object. It must be assumed, then, that Platonic existence implies an experience which supports this assertion—and it must be one which is ever recurring in history, for Plotinus and Augustine and the Platonism of the Renaissance and of the modern period say the same thing.

The question has already been touched on, how this philosophical attitude tallies with the concreteness of the Greek feeling for the body; and we said that it had nothing to do with true dualism, but rather presupposed just this vivacity of man's being. The Platonic intellectual life is the product of a double movement. The one movement starts from the body and its qualities as trained by gymnastics, from the artistically shaped world of forms, from an earthly reality permeated by politics, only to leave all that behind and to rise by an act felt as purely spiritual to the world of the Ideas, assumed to be just as purely spiritual. The other movement returns, with the insight into life and the fulness of values acquired there, to the terrestrial world, to reform it more in accordance with truth, in order that the next movement of knowledge may rise from it all the purer. The Platonic intellectual life thus has a dialectical character. In this lies its specific achievement; but from this too comes its danger. If the basis of form-endowed corporeality is lost sight of, the intellectual act loses itself in mere abstraction or in mystical unsubstantiality; if the ascent towards the spiritual is relaxed, the whole thing becomes aesthetic dilettantism. One is reminded of the apparently contradictory attitude of the *yoga* discipline, which requires that the neophyte whom it would lead to the transcendence of the mystical ascent shall be equipped with strong vitality and unimpaired power of enjoyment. In the same way the Platonic liberation presupposes as given that which is to be abandoned. It is a question then, after all, of the total man; only he is dissected, as it were, into a dialectical system, and the totality is realized in the counter-play of forces. Only when this dialectical counteraction and interaction breaks down does the danger become pressing.

For the rest, an ultimate humanity lies in this very tension. To man's deepest nature belongs the possibility of confronting that which touches his own sphere as a liminal value, namely pure spirit, and of making the perilous venture towards it. Freedom to venture forth into the extra-human is one of the most significant notes of man.

THE MAIN DISCOURSE
(Second Interlude)

CONSTERNATION

THE DIALOGUE has reached its first great climax, and the assembled company rests in the feeling of having achieved something great.

> *At these words there was a long silence. Socrates himself seemed to be absorbed in his argument, and so were most of us.*

Cebes and Simmias, however, are speaking in a low voice to one another. Socrates notices it. He sees that there is something still unsolved, and he likes the two intelligent critics; so he invites them to speak:

> *Simmias replied: Well, Socrates, I will tell you the truth. Each of us has a difficulty, and each has been pushing on the other, and urging him to ask you about it. We were anxious to hear what you have to say; but we were reluctant to trouble you, for we were afraid that it might be unpleasant to you to be asked questions now.*
>
> *Socrates smiled at this answer, and said, Dear me! Simmias, I shall find it hard to convince other people that I do not consider my fate a misfortune, when I cannot convince even you of it, and you are afraid that I am more peevish now than I used to be. You seem to think me inferior in prophetic power to the swans, which, when they find that they have to die, sing more loudly than they ever*

> sang before, for joy that they are about to depart into the presence of God, whose servants they are. The fear which men have of death themselves makes them speak falsely of the swans, and they say that the swan is wailing at its death, and that it sings loud for grief. They forget that no bird sings when it is hungry, or cold, or in any pain; not even the nightingale, nor the swallow, nor the hoopoe, which, they assert, wail and sing for grief. But I think that neither these birds nor the swan sing for grief. I believe that they have a prophetic power and foreknowledge of the good things in the next world, for they are Apollo's birds: and so they sing and rejoice on the day of their death, more than in all their life. And I believe that I myself am a fellow slave with the swans, and consecrated to the service of the same God, and that I have prophetic power from my master no less than they; and that I am not more despondent than they are at leaving this life. So, as far as vexing me goes, you may talk to me and ask questions as you please, as long as the Eleven of the Athenians will let you.

So begins the wonderful interlude, from which the flight of thought will grow grander and bolder. One feels what must have been the power of the man who had such clarity of thought, such grandeur of mind and so deep and lively a religious sense. One feels also what a fund of spiritual youthfulness must have been alive in the circle to which he could speak in such a manner.

Simmias answers:

> Good, said Simmias; I will tell you my difficulty, and Cebes will tell you why he is dissatisfied with your statement. I think, Socrates, and I daresay you think so too, that it is very difficult, and perhaps impossible, to obtain clear knowledge about these matters in this life. Yet I should hold him to be a very poor creature who did not test what is said about them in every way, and persevere until he had examined the question from every side, and could do no more. It is our duty to do one of two things. We must learn, or we must discover for ourselves, the truth of these matters; or, if that be impossible, we must take the best and most irrefragable of human doctrines, and embarking on that, as on a raft, risk the voyage of

life, unless a stronger vessel, some divine word, could be found, on which we might take our journey more safely and more securely.

This confidence of thought is fine; equally fine is the Master's reverence for truth and for the dignity of the seeking mind, to which no one must do violence—not even one who believes himself to have perfect insight. Simmias continues:

And now, after what you have said, I shall not be ashamed to put a question to you: and then I shall not have to blame myself hereafter for not having said now what I think. Cebes and I have been considering your argument; and we think that it is hardly sufficient.

I daresay you are right, my friend, said Socrates. But tell me, where is it insufficient?

Whereupon Simmias formulates his doubt.

To me it is insufficient, he replied, because the very same argument might be used of a harmony, and a lyre, and its strings. It might be said that the harmony in a tuned lyre is something unseen, and incorporeal, and perfectly beautiful, and divine, while the lyre and its strings are corporeal, and with the nature of bodies, and compounded, and earthly, and akin to the mortal. Now suppose that, when the lyre is broken and the strings are cut or snapped, a man were to press the same argument that you have used, and were to say that the harmony cannot have perished, and that it must still exist. . . .

And he again reinforces the argument very aptly:

And I think, Socrates, that you too must be aware that many of us believe the soul to be most probably a mixture and harmony of the elements by which our body is, as it were, strung and held together, such as heat and cold, and dry and wet, and the like, when they are mixed together well and in due proportion. Now if the soul is a harmony, it is clear that, when the body is relaxed out of proportion, or over-strung by disease or other evils, the soul, though most divine, must perish at once, like other harmonies of sound and of all works of art, while what remains of each body must remain for a long time, until it be burnt or rotted away. What then shall we say to a man who asserts that the soul, being a mixture of the elements of the body, perishes first, at what is called death?

Socrates now looked pensively before him, in the way he used to do so often, and with a gentle smile:

Simmias' objection is a fair one, he said. If any of you is readier than I am, why does he not answer? For Simmias looks like a formidable assailant. But before we answer him, I think that we had better hear what fault Cebes has to find with my reasoning, and so gain time to consider our reply. And then, when we have heard them both, we must either give in to them, if they seem to harmonize, or, if they do not, we must proceed to argue in defence of our reasoning. Come, Cebes, what is it that troubles you, and makes you doubt?

The other accordingly states his misgivings:

I will tell you, replied Cebes. I think that the argument is just where it was, and still open to our former objection. You have shown very cleverly, and, if it is not arrogant to say so, quite conclusively, that our souls existed before they entered the human form. I don't retract my admission on that point. But I am not convinced that they will continue to exist after we are dead. I do not agree with Simmias' objection, that the soul is not stronger and more lasting than the body: I think that it is very much superior in those respects. "Well, then," the argument might reply, "do you still doubt, when you see that the weaker part of a man continues to exist after his death? Do you not think that the more lasting part of him must necessarily be preserved for as long?" See, therefore, if there is anything in what I say; for I think that I, like Simmias, shall best express my meaning in a figure. It seems to me that a man might use an argument similar to yours, to prove that a weaver, who had died in old age, had not in fact perished, but was still alive somewhere; on the ground that the garment, which the weaver had woven for himself and used to wear, had not perished *or been destroyed. And if any one were incredulous, he might ask whether a human being, or a garment constantly in use and wear, lasts the longest; and on being told that a human being lasts much the longest, he might think that he had shown beyond all doubt that the man was safe, because what lasts a shorter time than the man had not perished. But that, I suppose, is not so, Simmias; for you too must examine what I say. Every one would understand that such an argument was simple nonsense. This weaver wove himself many such garments and wore them out; he outlived them all but the last, but he perished before that one. Yet a man is in no wise inferior to his cloak, or weaker than it, on that account. And I think that the soul's relation to the body may be expressed in a similar figure. Why should not a man very reasonably say in just the same way that the soul lasts a long time, while the body is weaker and lasts a shorter time? But, he might go on, each soul wears out many bodies, especially if she lives for many years. For if the body is in a state of flux and decay in the man's lifetime, and the soul is ever repairing the worn-out part, it will surely follow that the soul, on perishing, will be clothed in her last robe, and perish before that alone. But when the soul has perished, then the body will show its weakness and quickly rot away.*

Both objections are to be taken quite seriously. Simmias refers to the Pythagorean theory that the soul is the harmony of the body. If that is so, it does not exist as something in its own right, but only as the sum of the proportions and rhythms determining the body. The significance of this becomes clear at once if we translate it into the ideas of Nietzsche, for whom the body is not merely the biological element, but the human totality as such, certainly perishable, but even so full of an inexhaustible significance; while the soul, as the *Zarathustra* puts it, is "something about the body", the inward, musical aspect of it, therefore dying with it, or even before it.[1] That the theory makes a deep impression on Simmias, is easily understood. He is young and impressionable, and feels the power inherent in this combination of beauty and perishableness. What

[1] *Thus Spake Zarathustra*; "Zarathustra's Prologue, 6" and "On the Despisers of the Body".

Cebes says may be stated roughly as follows: That the soul which is under the influence of truth is stronger than the body, is evident; the only question is, whether this strengthening of the real by the valid, this irradiation of eternal power from the truth, is sufficient to overcome mortality altogether.

So the two objections in fact make a deep impression. How seriously Plato himself takes them is seen from the fact that the impression transmits itself also to the hearers of Phaedo's narrative, namely Echecrates and his friends. The framing device breaks into the narrative itself and makes the crisis of the conversation the principal pause in the whole action of the dialogue.

> *It made us all very uncomfortable to listen to them, as we afterwards said to each other. We had been fully convinced by the previous argument; and now they seemed to overturn our conviction, and to make us distrust all the arguments that were to come, as well as the preceding ones, and to doubt if our judgment was worth anything, or even if certainty could be attained at all.*

Phaedo has said "we", and Echecrates takes up the cue:

> *By the gods, Phaedo, I can understand your feelings very well. I myself felt inclined while you were speaking to ask myself, "Then what reasoning are we to believe in future? That of Socrates was quite convincing, and now it has fallen into discredit." For the doctrine that our soul is a harmony has always taken a wonderful hold of me, and your mentioning it reminded me that I myself had held it. And now I must begin again and find some other reasoning which shall convince me that a man's soul does not die with him at his death.*

He then becomes pressing:

> *So tell me, I pray you, how did Socrates pursue the argument? Did he show any signs of uneasiness, as you say that you did, or did he come to the defence of his argument calmly? And did he defend it satisfactorily or no? Tell me the whole story as exactly as you can.*

Encouragement

Phaedo is happy to be able to praise his master:

> *I have often, Echecrates, wondered at Socrates; but I never admired him more than I admired him then. There was nothing very strange in his having an answer: what I chiefly wondered at was, first, the kindness and good-nature and respect with which he listened to the young men's objections; and, secondly, the quickness with which he perceived their effect upon us; and, lastly, how well he healed our wounds, and rallied us as if we were beaten and flying troops, and encouraged us to follow him, and to examine the reasoning with him.*

One feels how the wonderful man prepares himself for a fresh effort—but the delicacy, nobility and strength with which this is done, strike the reader afresh every time he reads the passage.

> ECH. *How?*
>
> PHAEDO. *I will tell you. I was sitting by the bed on a stool at his right hand, and his seat was a good deal higher than mine. He stroked my head and gathered up the hair on my neck in his hand—you know he used often to play with my hair—and said, To-morrow, Phaedo, I daresay you will cut off these beautiful locks.*
>
> *I suppose so, Socrates, I replied.*
>
> *You will not, if you take my advice.*
>
> *Why not? I asked.*
>
> *You and I will cut off our hair to-day, he said, if our argument be dead indeed, and we cannot bring it to life again. And I, if I were you, and the argument were to escape me, would swear an oath, as the Argives did, not to wear my hair long again, until I had renewed the fight and conquered the argument of Simmias and Cebes.*
>
> *But Heracles himself, they say, is not a match for two, I replied.*
>
> *Then summon me to aid you, as your Iolaus,*[1] *while there is still light.*

---

[1] Iolaus was Heracles' armour-bearer.

Then I summon you, not as Heracles summoned Iolaus, but as Iolaus might summon Heracles.
It will be the same, he replied.

One of the deepest secrets, perhaps, of intellectual Greece was this intermingling of philosophic passion and human beauty. And this forms the starting-point for the brilliant advance which Socrates makes in the cause of thought in the next paragraphs, and which at the same time proves his mastery as a pedagogue.

But first let us take care not to make a mistake.
What mistake? I asked.
The mistake of becoming misologists, or haters of reasoning, as men become misanthropists, he replied: for to hate reasoning[1] is the greatest evil that can happen to us. Misology and misanthropy both come from similar causes. The latter arises out of the implicit and irrational confidence which is placed in a man, who is believed by his friend to be thoroughly true and sincere and trustworthy, and who is soon afterwards discovered to be a bad man and untrustworthy. This happens again and again; and when a man has had this experience many times, particularly at the hands of those whom he has believed to be his nearest and dearest friends, and he has quarrelled with many of them, he ends by hating all men, and thinking that there is no good at all in any one.

Socrates says, then: Before we begin work anew, we must clear up what has just happened. For something has in fact happened: we have experienced the collapse of a *logos* which we took to be reliable, and this collapse has, to your feeling, cast doubt on all enquiry and knowledge. We ought not to cover this up, we must get over it intellectually. We must take care that it gives rise to no mistrust of the significance and power of thought in general—as, for instance, when a man has given his confidence rashly, been deceived, and now regards all men as untrustworthy. Socrates pulls his disciples together, sharpens their critical vigilance, and anchors them in a deeper affirmation of the power of thought—this last

[1] The word *logoi* means spoken words, but also the problem stated in them, and the logical process by which it is discussed.

by showing them that a radical judgment as to good or bad seldom proves right. And a man who is disillusioned and denies the trustworthiness of any men, is incapable of dealing with men in the right way, much less of educating them.

> *Is it not clear that such a man tries to deal with men without understanding human nature? Had he understood it he would have known that, in fact, good men and bad men are very few indeed, and that the majority of men are neither one nor the other.*

The like holds good of thought and speech:

> *And, Phaedo, he said, if there be a system of reasoning which is true, and certain, and which our minds can grasp, it would be very lamentable that a man, who has met with some of these arguments which at one time seem true and at another false, should at last, in the bitterness of his heart gladly put all the blame on the reasoning, instead of on himself and his own unskilfulness, and spend the rest of his life in hating and reviling reasoning, and lose the truth and knowledge of reality.*
>
> *Indeed, I replied, that would be very lamentable.*

It follows from this:

> *First then, he said, let us be careful not to admit into our souls the notion that all reasoning is very likely unsound: let us rather think that we ourselves are not yet sound. And we must strive earnestly like men to become sound, you, my friends, for the sake of all your future life; and I, because of my death.*

He himself is in a peculiar position in this respect:

> *For I am afraid that at present I can hardly look at death like a philosopher; I am in a contentious mood, like the uneducated persons who never give a thought to the truth of the question about which they are disputing, but are only anxious to persuade their audience that they themselves are right. And I think that to-day I shall differ from them only in one thing. I shall not be anxious to persuade my audience that I am right, except by the way; but*

I shall be very anxious indeed to persuade myself. For see, my dear friend, how selfish my reasoning is. If what I say is true, it is well to believe it. But if there is nothing after death, at any rate I shall pain my friends less by my lamentations in the interval before I die. And this ignorance will not last for ever—that would have been an evil—it will soon come to an end. So prepared, Simmias and Cebes, he said, I come to the argument.

THE MAIN DISCOURSE
(*Third Part*)

THE ANSWER TO SIMMIAS

SOCRATES first recapitulates Simmias's objection. Then he recalls once more the fundamental thesis of Platonism, that all learning and knowledge is a reminiscence of something once seen, and that therefore the soul must have already existed before birth. The two friends assent; it is thus easy for him to show that Simmias's objection cannot be upheld:

You must choose which doctrine you will retain, that knowledge is recollection, or that the soul is a harmony.

The former, Socrates, certainly, he replied. The latter has never been demonstrated to me; it rests only on probable and plausible grounds, which make it a popular opinion. I know that doctrines which ground their proofs on probabilities are impostors, and that they are very apt to mislead, both in geometry and everything else, if one is not on one's guard against them.

But the disciples too are admonished of their responsibility.

And you, if you take my advice, will think not of Socrates, but of the truth; and you will agree with me, if you think that what I say is true: otherwise you will oppose me with every argument that you have: and be careful that, in my anxiety to convince you, I do not deceive both you and myself, and go away, leaving my sting behind me, like a bee.

Socrates confirms the refutation: If the soul were only the harmony of the body, two facts, which are yet undeniable, could not remain true. The first is that there is disharmony, contradiction and evil in the soul itself:

> *Or rather, Simmias, to speak quite accurately, I suppose that there will be no vice in any soul, if the soul is a harmony. I take it, there can never be any discord in a harmony, which is a perfect harmony.*

The second fact is that the soul can contradict the body, resist it, overcome it. It can do this really, and the more so the more living it is:

> *Well, now do we not find the soul acting in just the opposite way, and leading all the elements of which she is said to consist, and opposing them in almost everything all through life; and lording it over them in every way, and chastising them, sometimes severely, and with a painful discipline, such as gymnastic and medicine, and sometimes lightly; sometimes threatening and sometimes admonishing the desires and passions and fears, as though she were speaking to something other than herself, as Homer makes Odysseus do in the Odyssey, where he says that*
>
> > "*He smote upon his breast, and chid his heart:*
> > '*Endure, my heart, e'en worse hast thou endured.*'"
>
> *Do you think that when Homer wrote that, he supposed the soul to be a harmony, and capable of being led by the passions of the body, and not of a nature to lead them, and be their lord, being herself far too divine a thing to be like a harmony?*

THE ANSWER TO CEBES
AND THE DECISIVE ARGUMENT

The two young friends are Thebans, and Cebes is the cleverer; this explains the joke with which Socrates turns to the latter:

> *Very good, said Socrates; I think that we have contrived to appease our Theban Harmonia with tolerable success. But how*

about Cadmus, Cebes? he said. How shall we appease him, and with what reasoning?

If he has settled Harmonia, the wife of the founder of Thebes, perhaps he will have similar success with the stronger of the couple, namely Cadmus himself. Cebes begins to feel that it may not go well with his objection, and speaks guardedly:

I daresay that you will find out how to do it, said Cebes. At all events you have argued that the soul is not a harmony in a way which surprised me very much. When Simmias was stating his objection, I wondered how any one could possibly dispose of his argument: and so I was very much surprised to see it fall before the very first onset of yours. I should not wonder if the same fate awaited the argument of Cadmus.

But Socrates evidently takes his objection more seriously than that of Simmias; he recapitulates it fully, and then continues:

That, I think, Cebes, is the substance of your objection. I state it again and again on purpose, that nothing may escape us, and that you may add to it or take away from it anything that you wish.

The technique of the dialogue emphasizes the pause here by giving a glimpse of the Master's early life together with the scene of the last reunion:

Socrates paused for some time and thought. Then he said, It is not an easy question that you are raising, Cebes. We must examine fully the whole subject of the causes of generation and decay. If you like, I will give you my own experiences, and if you think that you can make use of anything that I say, you may employ it to satisfy your misgivings.

And now there is a sort of review of his own intellectual development; facing death, he gives an account of his philosophic way. We must leave to itself the question what biographical importance the account has; part of it is probably correct in this sense too. In the dialogue, at any rate, it marks the genesis of the Platonic figure of Socrates.

> *Listen, then, and I will tell you, Cebes, he replied. When I was a young man, I had a passionate desire for the wisdom which is called Physical Science. I thought it a splendid thing to know the causes of everything; why a thing comes into being, and why it perishes, and why it exists. I was always worrying myself with such questions as, Do living creatures take a definite form, as some persons say, from the fermentation of heat and cold? Is it the blood, or the air, or fire by which we think? Or is it none of these, but the brain which gives the senses of hearing and sight and smell, and do memory and opinion come from these, and knowledge from memory and opinion when in a state of quiescence?*

But he then loses confidence in all these speculations:

> *Again, I used to examine the destruction of these things, and the changes of the heaven and the earth until at last I concluded that I was wholly and absolutely unfitted for these studies. I will prove that to you conclusively. I was so completely blinded by these studies, that I forgot what I had formerly seemed to myself and to others to know quite well: I unlearnt all that I had been used to think that I understood; even the cause of man's growth. Formerly I had thought it evident on the face of it that the cause of growth was eating and drinking; and that, when from food flesh is added to flesh, and bone to bone, and in the same way to the other parts of the body their proper elements, then by degrees the small bulk grows to be large, and so the boy becomes a man. Don't you think that my belief was reasonable?*
>
> *I do, said Cebes.*
>
> *Then here is another experience for you. I used to feel no doubt, when I saw a tall man standing by a short one, that the tall man was, it might be, a head the taller, or, in the same way, that one horse was bigger than another. I was even clearer that ten was more than eight by the addition of two, and that a thing two cubits long was longer by half its length than a thing one cubit long.*
>
> *And what do you think now? asked Cebes.*
>
> *I think that I am very far from believing that I know the cause of any of these things. Why, when you add one to one, I am not sure either that the one to which one is added has become two, or*

that the one added and the one to which it is added become, by the addition, two.

What the problem consists in is made clear by some examples, of which the last is particularly impressive:

I cannot understand how, when they are brought together, this union, or placing of one by the other, should be the cause of their becoming two, whereas, when they were separated, each of them was one, and they were not two. Nor, again, if you divide one into two, can I convince myself that this division is the cause of one becoming two: for then a thing becomes two from exactly the opposite cause. In the former case it was because two units were brought together, and the one was added to the other; while now it is because they are separated, and the one divided from the other.

So the consequence is:

Nor, again, can I persuade myself that I know how one is generated; in short, this method does not show me the cause of the generation or destruction or existence of anything: I have in my own mind a confused idea of another method, but I cannot admit this one for a moment.

By this method, says Socrates, one cannot know "the cause of the generation or destruction or existence of anything". More precisely: why anything begins or ceases to be, or exists, as this particular thing. The question is concerned, then, not with being real, but with being this; not with a thing's presence or absence, but with its nature. The empirical method cannot explain this. So Socrates seeks further, and hits on the Philosophy of Nature:

But one day I listened to a man who said that he was reading from a book of Anaxagoras, which affirmed that it is Mind which orders and is the cause of all things. I was delighted with this theory; it seemed to me to be right that mind should be the cause of all things, and I thought to myself, If this is so, then mind will order and arrange each thing in the best possible way. So if we wish to discover the cause of the generation or destruction or existence of a thing, we must discover how it is best for that thing to exist, or to act, or to be acted on.

If Reason is the principle of all things, the meaning and cause of every phenomenon will be found by asking what is the best possible state in which it can be conceived—its ontological and logical optimum. This "best", as evident in its necessity of significance, is the nature of the case in question, and the only satisfactory philosophy is to refer the phenomenon to it—a vigorous statement of rational absolutism, for which the rationally evident is also the worthily valid, and both identical with the essentially existent. The true, the good, and that which is, are ultimately one.

> *I thought that he would assign a cause to each thing, and a cause to the universe, and then would go on to explain to me what was best for each thing, and what was the common good of all. I would not have sold my hopes for a great deal: I seized the books very eagerly, and read them as fast as I could, in order that I might know what is best and what is worse.*

But he was disappointed:

> *All my splendid hopes were dashed to the ground, my friend, for as I went on reading I found that the writer made no use of Mind at all, and that he assigned no causes for the order of things. His causes were air, and ether, and water, and many other strange things.*

He tries to explain by an example what the disappointment consisted in:

> *I thought that he was exactly like a man who should begin by saying that Socrates does all that he does by Mind, and who, when he tried to give a reason for each of my actions, should say, first, that I am sitting here now, because my body is composed of bones and muscles, and that the bones are hard and separated by joints, while the muscles can be tightened and loosened, and, together with the flesh, and the skin which holds them together, cover the bones; and that therefore, when the bones are raised in*

their sockets, the relaxation and contraction of the muscles makes it possible for me now to bend my limbs, and that that is the cause of my sitting here with my legs bent. And in the same way he would go on to explain why I am talking to you: he would assign voice, and air, and hearing, and a thousand other things as causes; but he would quite forget to mention the real cause, which is that since the Athenians thought it right to condemn me, I have thought it right and just to sit here and to submit to whatever sentence they may think fit to impose. For, by the dog of Egypt, I think that these muscles and bones would long ago have been in Megara or Boeotia, prompted by their opinion of what is best, if I had not thought it better and more honourable to submit to whatever penalty the state inflicts, rather than escape by flight. But to call these things causes is too absurd! If it were said that without bones and muscles and the other parts of my body I could not have carried my resolutions into effect, that would be true. But to say that they are the cause of what I do, and that in this way I am acting by Mind, and not from choice of what is best, would be a very loose and careless way of talking.

By this road, then, no real answer was obtained; so he had to take another road:

That danger occurred to me. I was afraid that my soul might be completely blinded if I looked at things with my eyes, and tried to grasp them with my senses. So I thought that I must have recourse to conceptions[1] and examine the truth of existence by means of them.

He then explains this in more detail:

I mean nothing new, he said; only what I have repeated over and over again, both in our conversation to-day and at other times. I am going to try to explain to you the kind of cause at which I have worked, and I will go back to what we have so often spoken of, and begin with the assumption that there exists an absolute beauty, and an absolute good, and an absolute greatness, and so on. If

[1] *Logoi*: see note 1, p. 139.

you grant me this, and agree that they exist, I hope to be able to show you what my cause is, and to discover that the soul is immortal.

You may assume that I grant it you, said Cebes; go on with your proof.

Then do you agree with me in what follows? he asked. It appears to me that if anything besides absolute beauty is beautiful, it is so simply because it partakes of absolute beauty, and I say the same of all phenomena. Do you allow that kind of cause?

I do, he answered.

Well then, he said, I no longer recognize, nor can I understand, these other wise causes: if I am told that anything is beautiful because it has a rich colour, or a goodly form, or the like, I pay no attention, for such language only confuses me; and in a simple and plain, and perhaps a foolish way, I hold to the doctrine that the thing is only made beautiful by the presence or communication, or whatever you please to call it, of absolute beauty.

What does all this mean?

Socrates had been confronted with the fundamental questions of philosophy: "What is that which is? How is it what it is? What makes it what it is?" With these questions he went to the philosophers of Nature, who had proclaimed that they treated everything by reason, that is, scientifically. It turned out, however, that they understood by this the reference of empirical phenomena to ultimate, metaphysically conceived constituents, such as water, air, fire, and so forth—that they practised, therefore, a kind of mythological physics—and Socrates got no answer to his questions. What he wanted to know was not, what things were made up of and into what they were resolved again, but what that was in them which came out to meet the receptive mind with such peculiar impressiveness: their nature, their meaning-complex, that about them which was absolute. This cannot be deduced from any analysis of their component parts—any more than the meaning of his own fate, of his present sojourn in prison, can be deduced from the fact that his bones and sinews are constructed in such and such a way and that consequently he is sitting on his bed in this posture. He wants to know by what structure of nature and meaning the matter and energy of experience, in their composition and dissolution, are justified by the standards of mind. He is not in prison because his body is anatomically built in such and such a way—we might add: because the chain holds him fast, because the court has condemned him, because political events at Athens have put the conservatives in power—but because, from his insight into the ethical significance of what has happened to him, he has considered it his duty to remain rather than to escape. Because he has come to see clearly the ethical *eidos* which contains both the imperative, that which ought to be, and the "best" for himself, that is, the meaningful. Accordingly he does not want to know what physical or physiological processes are at work in the impression of the beautiful, but in what consists that complex of essence and significance which affects us powerfully, elevates and makes us happy, in the consciousness of a beautiful thing. It is the philosophical question as such, then, that he states; and we admire the exemplary clarity with which it is stated.

But how is this question answered? How could it be answered? Perhaps in a subjective sense, by saying that the significant content of things, what is categorical in them, is derived from the human mind itself, or from consciousness in general as realized therein, in the manner of idealistic apriorism. In that case only the mass of perceptions is given "from outside"; meaning is brought into them by the classifying activity of the mind itself. Or one could follow Aristotle and say that things themselves are constructed on a categorical scheme. Man grasps them by sense-perception; the abstractive power of his mind extracts the essential structure from the percept and formulates it in the concept. Neither of these two answers would satisfy Plato. The former would not, because his experience of mental synthesis is too elementary to justify him in demolishing the reality of the world so radically as it does. The latter answer would not satisfy him, because something is urgent in him which the Aristotelian type of mind lacks: that peculiar craving for perfection and completeness, which at once removes it from the empirical with its incompleteness and inadequacy. To put it still more radically: that particular experience of what is called "essence", of the meaning-force of the qualitative complex, its symbolic power and force of validity, by which the Platonic amazement is aroused. Only from this fundamental experience can the Platonic questions and answers in the last resort be understood.

So Plato must give a different answer. He says that each thing exhibits a certain stock of qualities, relations, arrangements and values, which necessarily gives the impression of validity. But on the other hand the imperfection, fragmentariness and perishability of the thing will not allow us to regard that validity as resting in the thing itself, but point beyond it. The sense-quality of the thing declares itself as secondary, and points to something primary which is connected with it and yet independent of it: a significant form free from all limitation, realizing all its consequences, immune from all defilements—the *eidos*, the Idea. This dwells in an eternal sphere, remote from all limitation and change; the thing, on the other hand, in the restrictedness and mutability of earthly conditions. What essence and meaning it contains, derives from the Idea: it participates in this.

If, then, it is asked what something is, the answer is: It is, in the form of participation, what its Idea is in the form of originality and essentiality. If one asks why it is what it is, the answer will be: because its Idea constitutes it such. The further question, however, why the Idea is as it is, and why it is at all, receives the answer: because it is so. Its being so is an original phenomenon, and as such absolute as well as evident. As soon as the Idea is really beheld, the question ceases. Why is this human being beautiful? Not because certain proportions of bone-structure or a certain state of tissue and skin are found in him, but because he participates in the Idea of the Beautiful. But the Idea of the Beautiful is "the Beautiful itself"; the original phenomenon of beauty, which as soon as it shines forth clearly convinces by itself. The question remains only in the region of things, which are not the Beautiful itself, but only participate in it, and are therefore imperfect and perishable; questioning comes to rest in the contemplation of the Beautiful Itself. All else, the various concrete cases of a physical, biological, sociological or historical nature are for this question secondary. They represent only the forms in which is actualized the fact which alone furnishes the true answer: that the Idea of the Beautiful is shown forth in the thing.

Each thing has its meaning above itself. It exists upwards and from above. Hence arises that tension between the empirical and the real which is superior to it; that urge towards the absolute, which is peculiar to Plato, the liveliness and seriousness of which is expressed in the conception of Eros.

> *Again, you would be careful not to affirm that, if one is added to one, the addition is the cause of two, or, if one is divided, that the division is the cause of two? You would protest loudly that you know of no way in which a thing can be generated, except by participation in its own proper essence; and that you can give no cause for the generation of two except participation in duality; and that all things which are to be two must participate in duality, while whatever is to be one must participate in unity. You would leave the explanation of these divisions and additions and all such subtleties to wiser men than yourself. . . . But you, I think, if you are a philosopher, will do as I say.*
>
> *Very true, said Simmias and Cebes together.*

This final assent is echoed—as were the foregoing misgivings—by Phaedo's hearers, Echecrates and his friends.

> ECH. *And they were right, Phaedo. I think the clearness of his reasoning, even to the dullest, is quite wonderful.*
>
> PHAEDO. *Indeed, Echecrates, all who were there thought so too.*
>
> ECH. *So do we who were not there, but who are listening to your story.*

The question was asked: why is this horse beautiful?—and the answer was: because it participates in the Idea of the Beautiful. Does not this way of thinking by-pass the investigation of the case and instead hypostatize mere words? This would be so if it were not related to a specific experience. This experience is so important that it may be characterized once again.

One who thinks Platonically forms a peculiar conception of the system of qualities belonging to a being, for example a horse, or of one of these qualities singly, for example beauty. A complex of qualities as well as a single quality appear to him not as determinations which, even though abstractly conceivable, yet according to their reality are entirely inherent in the thing, but as self-constituted significant forms which detach themselves from the thing. They are perfect, belong to the ideal order, and are exempt from the contingent, damaged and distorted world of the senses. Their force of validity is so great that it outweighs the reality of the empirical, nay, to the feeling of those who experience it, takes on the character of a higher reality. This is what Plato seems to mean when he says that the Idea is "that which really is". The nature of this super-reality is no doubt hard to define. The meaning of the Idea is differently defined in the different epochs of Platonic thought; it ranges from the symbolic expression of logical concepts to the notion of independent essences. Without attempting to exhaust it in any way, perhaps the following remarks may be made.

The Ideas are the point at which the question "what is ?" finally arrives: that is, the essential simply. They are likewise the goal of the question "what ought to be ? what is worthy to be ? whence has the worthy its value ?": that is, the valid simply. And these Ideas are images too. Not concepts or principles which are abstractly thought by the understanding, but forms which are beheld by the mind's eye. For Plato the ultimately real in existence consists neither in atomistic elements nor in formal laws. The knowledge-seeking investigation of this existence ends, not in logical combinations of characteristics, but in significant figures. All that is capable of being experienced leads back to such figures. Every single quality, for instance velocity or purity of tone, has its *eidos*; likewise things, for example the horse or the lyre. These significant figures are images of essence in so far as they answer the question as to quality, images of value in so far as they answer the question as to dignity.

The Ideas are not merely symbolically conceived logical concepts or categorical forms, but something objective, self-subsistent. This follows already from the Platonic doctrine that all knowing is reminiscence, so that a man confronted with an object becomes aware that he has once, before his birth, contemplated its significant content, namely the Idea. The ideas do not depend on things, but form self-based articulations of validity. As little does their perception depend on that of things. Of course, anyone who is to perceive the nature of a horse must meet a horse, but only in order that this encounter may provide the occasion for the Idea once contemplated to light up before his mind. The Ideas of qualities, species, relations, and so forth, form an eternal cosmos lying above the world of things, and this is the true object of the mind, of its knowledge, appreciation and effort.

It is very difficult to answer the question, in what manner the Idea is "there". The notions immediately available are those of reality and validity. The concrete, which meets the empirical thrust of my own concrete being, is real.[1] A logical law or an ethical norm, which my judgment and conscience perceive as binding, is valid. But a third form of the given seems to be attributed to the Idea, a form in which reality and validity coincide. It is a fundamental feeling among Platonists that reality is not a uniform predicate; it is not simply the fact, predicable of any and every object, that it is, instead of not being; reality has various degrees—and indeed an infinite number of them. The degree of reality that belongs to a being—apart from the rank of the significant content itself, which does not come into consideration here—depends on how far it realizes its Idea. It is not real simply, and on top of that more or less perfect; on the contrary, the degree of its reality corresponds to the measure in which it fulfils its essence. This line of signification points to something that needs no further realization, since it actuates the full content of its essence and value, and thereby attains complete reality: the Idea. It is at once wholly valid and real, "that which simply is". There is here, of course, a problem; and Plato too seems to be aware of it. For the identity of validity and reality constitutes a form of being which can in strictness only be attributed to the Absolute. The Idea, however, is indeed "absolute", because simply valid; but it is not "the Absolute", since it does not exhaust the whole content of validity, but rather limits it. Thus the statement that it is that which simply is, is after all not quite correct; and

[1] The modern man inclines to regard only material things as real, equating "mind" with "thought", or rather with "thought-content", though the latter is not real but imagined. In fact, the mind is thoroughly real; it is even, in a sense still to be defined, more real than corporal things.

the necessary implication of meaning leads in fact to the Idea's being reinforced by the Absolute in the true sense, namely the Good. Of this more anon.

The general character of the Platonic approach involves the danger of seeing in things the corrupting principle of the Ideas, of regarding this corruption as implied by matter, and of representing the origin of things by a dualistic myth about the downfall of spirit into matter. And in fact we find in Platonic philosophy rudiments which point in this direction; though, as already pointed out, there can be no question of a true dualism. The original power of vision and construction, the will to form the given, the impulses to train the right kind of man and, as the sum of human things, the right kind of State, are so strong that they do not admit of any fundamental rejection of matter. From this results a fluctuating condition, in which the inclination to see Idea and mind as the only reality and sensible things as a degradation, is counterbalanced by the will to see things as co-ordinated with the Ideas, and the purpose of action as the earthly realization of the latter. Thus the thing, after all, stands in a positive relation to the Idea. It has a real content of essence and value, though this is derived not from itself but from the Idea. The relation is expressed in various ways: the thing portrays the Idea, or participates in the Idea, or the Idea is present in it, so that the contemplating mind can be reminded by it of what it once gazed on in the life before birth. The rank of the thing, as already remarked, is in each case determined by the measure in which it participates in its Idea.

It follows from all this that the Idea is in close relation with knowledge, that it has to do with truth. It is emphasized again and again that it forms the true object of cognition. Knowledge as such is the contemplation of the Idea; truth as such is the emergence of the Idea in the mind's gaze. This does not mean, however, that the seeker after knowledge must betake himself to a region of abstruse, purely inward contemplation. He must of course leave the senses behind and seek the Idea with purely spiritual sight; but he may, nay must, remain in contact with things. These are indeed mere copies of the genuine, and not in the true sense real; but on the other hand they *are* copies after all, and as such have a share in that from which they are copied. So they too can be known; and the knowable in them is in fact just their relation to the Idea and their ideal content. The Idea, therefore, forms not only the true object of knowledge, but also that by which the thing becomes open and penetrable to the contemplating gaze. The Idea turns the lump of earthly half-reality into an object of knowledge, that is, into truth. The Idea—and every Idea—is the possibility of lighting up the dark, fluctuating, earthly being. This is expressed also in the close relation which it has to light. He who looks on things merely with the bodily senses "grows blind in soul"; the light which makes the soul see, and is at the same time itself the object of sight, is the Idea. "Light"—the symbol runs through all Western thought—denotes the intellect and intellectual acts: more precisely, intellectual acts in so far as they realize the valid, the true, the beautiful, and so forth. Thus the Ideas are figures of light; they show how the world and the things of the world become visible, estimable, comprehensible by the intellectual act. The notion of light is always recurring in Plato, and reaches its climax in the doctrine of the Good. The *Republic* demonstrates in detail that the eyesight and the object with its qualities are not by themselves sufficient for vision to take place, but that "a third thing, specially appointed for this purpose", must be added, namely light. (507d–e.) Now, what the sun is for the bodily eyes, the Good is for the intellectual. So we read in the same context: "This, then, which gives truth to things known, and power (of knowing) to the knower, shall be called the Idea of the Good. Regard it as that which is the cause of knowledge and truth, so far as this is perceived (not by the external senses, but) by the mind . . ." The faculty of knowledge and the object of knowledge are not themselves the Good; this must rather be regarded as "something other and still fairer than they". (508e.) The true and ultimate light, the sun of the intellectual realm, is the Good. From it both the intellectual act of knowing and its object, the Idea, get their character of luminosity.

This leads us to the religious character of the Idea, and gives us occasion once more to take up the problem which has been indicated in its general lines. In the first place, the Idea is something ultimate: that in which the acts of cognition, evaluation, and so forth, end. If the Idea is beheld and appreciated, then truth is found, the valid is affirmed, the valuable is realized. These statements, however, are backed by a further argument at the end of the Sixth and beginning of the Seventh Books of the *Republic*. (It must be added at once that the word "argument" does not sufficiently designate what is meant. As the whole style and tone of the passage shows, it is a question of something uttermost, which cannot be stated openly in words, but only guessed at and revered with awe and emotion.) Socrates says, then: Material light makes the object visible, and the eye capable of seeing. There is correspondingly an intellectual light, the Good, which sets the intellectual faculty of knowledge and its object, that is, mind and Idea, in the cognitive relation. Both knowledge and truth are "beautiful"—the supreme expression for positive valuation —; but that Light itself "is something different and even more beautiful than they". It would no doubt be "correct to consider them both as of the nature of good",[1] but not "to regard either of them as the Good itself; rather must the essential nature of the Good be esteemed still higher". The partner in the dialogue answers with emotion: "The beauty you speak of is an immeasurable one"—but Socrates says warningly: "Be silent!"[2] The passage which follows next says still more about the Good: it gives to things not only the possibility of being known, but also their "being and essence".[3] "The Good itself, however, is not essence, but surpasses even essence in dignity and power." And Glaucon again replies with a cry of emotion: "O Apollo, what a divine excess!" (509a–c.) The Ideas are the presuppositions of all cognition, but are themselves "without hypothesis" and "the origin of everything"; they are the significant figures of the world; the essential images, which disclose the mystery of existence to knowledge (511b). They are an ultimate, then, behind which it should be impossible to go further back. And yet there is still something behind them; an Uttermost, by which they in their turn have truth and being, validity and reality: namely the

---

[1] *Agathoeidês*: that which has the essential nature of the good.
[2] A word from the language of the Mysteries: *euphêmei* means, originally, "speak words of good omen", in order that the sacred action may be happily accomplished. But as there was no security that the words would be really of good omen, the sense became changed to "keep a devout silence".
[3] *Ousia*, in the fuller sense, which combines "essence" with "being", the *quid* with the *quod*.

Good. This Good is represented by the image of the sun, and it is in the nature of the sun that things are seen in its light, but that it cannot itself be gazed on without injury. So the image denotes an inaccessibility, which recurs in speculative terms—in the passage where it is said that the Good indeed gives to knowledge the power to know, to truth the character of truth, to the ultimately essential and existent essence and being, but that itself it is more than all this. As in the image of the sun the object is veiled from the eyes by the excess of the very element which is the presupposition of seeing, namely light: so here the intellectual object is withdrawn from thought by the excess of just that which is the presupposition of thinking, and thereby an absolute transcendence produced; for there remains no category for that which lies above truth, essence and being. What is the meaning of all this? First, the Platonic conception of Good must be made clear in all its force. It is not a particular form of value standing beside others—the True, the Beautiful, and the Just—but is worthiness in general; that which is to be esteemed, affirmed and sought simply; significance in its final fulness and validity. And not merely as the object of an intellectual act—shall we say, of a fundamental, original and total affirmation behind all partial affirmations—but as a religious mystery, only to be approached by the cry of reverent wonder and the silence of awe-struck veneration. With regard more particularly to the relation of the Good to the Ideas, this is equally mysterious and equally transcends the possibility of conceptual statement, for it includes the above-mentioned antinomy. On the one hand the Idea is the essential and existent, the object of knowledge as such, and so requires no further reduction or reason. It is valid because it is valid, is because it is, and therefore constitutes the ultimate for the objectively referred act of cognition and evaluation. Yet there is a reference beyond it. It is indeed simply valid, but limited, and therefore not all-comprehensive; it is indeed absolute, but not the Absolute itself, rather a refraction of this, a step it takes towards the finite. The Idea of Justice is, simply as such, not that of Courage; between them there is distinction and so delimitation. But behind them lies the Absolute simply, which is also the All-inclusive. It is no longer an "image", but excels every image; it is not the subject of a particular proposition, but lies beyond every particular proposition. To keep within the phraseology of the dialogue, it is the "Sun", "Light" simply, the significance of which does not consist in being contemplated, but in enabling the images to be contemplated and the corresponding particular propositions to be made about them. This mysterious character of the Good comes out also in the Ideas. To behold them, therefore, is not merely a philosophical, but a religious act. The Idea is an eternal essence full of numinous significance, and to approach it means to approach also the source of this significance, namely the Good. In the contemplation of the particular Idea the Good is contemplated and experienced along with it, and the statements about its meaning only acquire their full sense when this religious experience is taken together with them.

As for the problems concerned with particular things, these are in no way affected by the reference to the Ideas, but must be worked out in connection with the respective data themselves. The theory of the Idea supersedes neither empirical nor phenomenological research, but only brings these into a metaphysical coherence which is attested by specific experience.

There follows now in the dialogue a somewhat complicated train of thought, which leads from the notion of the Idea to the general object of the whole exposition. According to this each Idea has an absolute power of self-assertion and self-differentiation. It will not tolerate that anything included under its definition shall at the same time be included under that of another Idea: the expression, in terms of the Idea-theory, of the principles of identity and contradiction.

> *It seems to me not only that absolute greatness will never be great and small at once, but also that greatness in us[1] never admits smallness, and will not be exceeded. One of two things must happen: either the greater will give way and fly at the approach of its opposite, the less, or it will perish. It will not stand its ground, and receive smallness, and be other than it was.*

---

[1] That is, the greatness of a concrete being, for example, our own body, in contradistinction from greatness in itself.

Every qualitative definition differentiates itself from another with an energy which is represented by the image of a conflict for life and death. Important too is the next argument, according to which one quality does not originate from another, but can only come into being or cease. Every true quality is an original phenomenon and therefore underivable. Hereupon one of the company objects that according to the former statements everything originates from its opposite, so for example the state of being dead from that of being alive, and *vice versa*:

> *Socrates inclined his head to the speaker and listened. Well and bravely remarked, he said: but you have not noticed the difference between the two propositions. What we said then was that a concrete thing is generated from its opposite: what we say now is that the absolute opposite can never become opposite to itself, either when it is in us, or when it is in nature. We were speaking then of things in which the opposites are, and we named them after those opposites: but now we are speaking of the opposites themselves, whose inherence gives the things their names; and they, we say, will never be generated from each other.*

Things, concrete figures endowed with qualities, can originate from one another, for example, a dead thing from a living one; but not the qualities as such; not, then, the state of being dead, considered in itself, from the state of being alive, similarly considered. These predicates, on the contrary, differ from one another with the specific energy of quality. That "becoming", therefore, which manifests itself in relation to them, must be understood otherwise. The argument is not easy, and Socrates does well to make sure that he is understood:

> *At the same time he turned to Cebes and asked, Did his objection trouble you at all, Cebes?*
>
> *No, replied Cebes; I don't feel that difficulty. But I will not deny that many other things trouble me.*
>
> *Then we are quite agreed on this point, he said. An opposite will never be opposite to itself.*
>
> *No, never, he replied.*

Now there are statements which imply other statements. For example, if I say that something falls under the numerical Idea of three, I have thereby also said that it is odd.

> *You know, I think, that whatever the idea of three is in, is bound to be not three only, but odd as well.*
> *Certainly.*
> *Well, we say that the opposite idea to the form which produces this result will never come to that thing.*
> *Indeed, no.*
> *But the idea of the odd produces it?*
> *Yes.*
> *And the idea of the even is the opposite of the idea of the odd?*
> *Yes.*
> *Then the idea of the even will never come to three?*
> *Certainly not.*
> *So three has no part in the even?*
> *None.*
> *Then the number three is uneven?*
> *Yes.*

The Idea of trinity necessarily imports into everything of which it takes possession the further predicate of oddness.

Socrates then starts afresh:

> *Then, he went on, tell me, what is that which must be in a body to make it alive?*
> *A soul, he replied.*
> *And is this always so?*
> *Of course, he said.*
> *Then the soul always brings life to whatever contains her?*
> *No doubt, he answered.*
> *And is there an opposite to life, or not?*
> *Yes.*
> *What is it?*
> *Death.*

And we have already agreed that the soul cannot ever receive the opposite of what she brings?
Yes, certainly we have, said Cebes.

That is to say: the predicate of being alive is related to that of being a soul, as the predicate of being odd is related to that of being three. That which is soul is also necessarily alive. This is in fact stated at once and expressly:

Well; what name did we give to that which does not admit the idea of the even?
The uneven, he replied.
And what do we call that which does not admit justice or music?
The unjust, and the unmusical.
Good; and what do we call that which does not admit death?
The immortal, he said.
And the soul does not admit death?
No.
Then the soul is immortal?
It is.
Good, he said. Shall we say that this is proved? What do you think?
Yes, Socrates, and very sufficiently.

Here the train of thought concludes. This is what has been said: Being alive is a necessary predicate of that which is soul. It belongs to its nature. But what belongs to a thing's nature cannot not be. Therefore the soul cannot be dead, and so cannot die.

The Force of the Argument

It is clear that there is no question of a proof here. If Socrates wished to prove that the soul is immortal, he would have to go about it in a different way. For instance, he would have to ask: Is there a kind of living being which by its origin, development, behaviour, by the content of its actions and the tenor of its whole being, gives the impression of entire mortality, and actually dissolves completely after a time? This is so, in the case of animals. But what about the life-principle of man? Does it differ from that of animals? Not by its mere biological structure, as, for example, cold-blooded animals differ from warm-blooded, or mammals from birds, but by a different kind of origin and a different character of actions, of self-possession and of relations with other beings, a difference in the whole bearing and sense of his existence? There is such a difference of quality, not degree, and it must have its root in being. What is the reality in question? The answer must be: the spirit. Not merely a spiritual principle, such as determines every being, but the substantial spiritual soul. The vital manifestations of this soul would now have to be analysed more closely, and it would have to be asked what inferences as to its nature could be drawn from them. It would further be seen that it cannot be destroyed by any conceivable cause, but is exempt from death by virtue of its nature. A proof of this kind is not even attempted, but Socrates starts from the Idea of the soul and says: This Idea is that of life as such; therefore it cannot include the predicate "dead" in its connotation. So the soul has nothing in common with death, but is immortal.

It might be objected that there is nothing more than an analytical judgment in question here. First the notion of an absolute life is constructed, then a characteristic feature included in it is taken out and without any justification applied to reality. Such a naïve procedure, however, can hardly be credited to Plato; rather, there is missing from the exposition a link which is self-evident to the speaker. The Idea of the soul is not constructed, but dawns on the thinker from experience of his inward life, as the *eidos* of the latter. The speaker here is a Greek, most intensely sensitive to the fact of mortality. He sees that everything falls a prey to this mortality; but within himself he discovers something—the soul—which is different from all that dies. He does not invent this, nor does he conjecture it, but perceives it. As he sees it in the face of other men, by virtue of their expression, so he sees it too inside himself: in the experience of cognition, in the process by which values are sought and found, in the moral conflict and its mastery, and so forth. In these processes he grasps the soul, sees it, hears it, feels it. In all this it is not a matter of subjective feeling, but of the "given process" of genuine experience, real encounter with that which is. This entity is distinct from everything corporeal: it is neither extended nor composite; it is rich, strong, creative, but at the same time simple and not to be taken hold of by any physical means. So too it lives in a different manner from all other living things, including one's own body. Its life is not given to it by generation and birth, nor maintained by material food, but has a peculiar originality and independence. It is spirit; living in the body and yet distinct from it; correlative to it and yet, as is seen for instance in the facts of self-condemnation and self-mastery, sovereign over it. From all this shines forth the Idea of a living being whose life flows in a unique manner from its nature.[1] This Idea is looked on as the manifestation of that peculiar vitality which is experienced within oneself—just as the latter is illuminated in turn by the apparition and evolution of that *eidos*. And now begins the analysis of the Idea thus discovered; not by any means a transference of unreal or conceptual elements to the real, obliterating boundaries, but the legitimate development of a meaning-complex which rests on a corresponding experience of being and shines forth ever anew from this.

There is a second consideration: the philosopher perceives that the soul's vitality is not merely of a substantial nature. The soul is not living in the same way, for example, as water is flowing. That too is true perhaps, in the sense of the simple indestructibility of the soul, but there is more than that: the vitality of the soul is rather at once a fact given and a task set, and realizes itself in the attitude to truth, to justice, in a word, to that which ought to be. The moment it strives after truth, it becomes like truth, and therein consists the truly spiritual vitality and reality of the soul. This is the purer and stronger, the more entirely the soul devotes itself to truth, the more decisively it wills the good. The philosopher recognizes this and makes it the foundation of his existence. He distinguishes the value-conditioned vitality and reality of the soul from that of the body, the biological; but also from the merely ontological vitality and

---

[1] This impression is so strong that it is exaggerated—in the doctrine of the spiritual soul's existence before birth—into that of absoluteness. The soul appears so essentially living that it is declared to be not only immortal but uncreated, not only indestructible but necessary. Here occurs that fatal shift which is characteristic of idealism; "spirit" is made equivalent to "absolute spirit".

reality of the soul as spiritual substance; he develops it in the continual effort after truth, and for the sake of this life makes the sacrifice of everything else. He lives resigned to the death of that which is only transitorily alive, in order that the eternally alive may flourish. By his doing this the *eidos* of the life in question here becomes ever clearer to him—that of immortal life in general, as also that of his own immortality. This awareness is not "experience" or "faith" in any irresponsible or subjective sense, but the becoming attentive to a specific reality and the recognition of a task set thereby. At the outset is the readiness to see what is. In the act of seeing, the object to be seen comes out more boldly, and therewith the possibility of intellectual analysis. Under this influence the organ of perception is again strengthened, making new and better vision possible—and so on. It is a matter, then, of a whole: a combination and interaction of object, organ and act; of datum, task and growth—it is a matter of philosophical existence.

A third consideration: the experience of the indestructibility of mind bears a religious character. The analysis of the Idea, as remarked above, comes up against a peculiar antinomy: on the one hand the Idea rests on itself, since it is a significant form of absolute validity; on the other hand it points beyond itself, since it is not the absolutely valid as such, but a form, and therefore something limited. So it has its roots in something that is definitive and ultimate, the Good. This Good has a thoroughly numinous nature; it is the proper divinity of the Platonic world. It emerges in every Idea; and if the Idea is the significant form in which entity becomes manifest and apprehensible by the intellectual act, it is also at the same time the form by which entity is lifted into the light of the eternal mystery. When, therefore, the perception of the Idea—and of the thing in its Idea—is performed in accordance with philosophical requirement, it merges into a religious act, and the result of the perception, namely truth, acquires the character of a religious intuition. It is this that gives the conversations of the dialogue that peculiar pathos which makes them other and more than a mere philosophizing in the modern specialist sense. The immortality of the soul is looked at from the standpoint of the numinous power of the Eternal Good. This power is able to give to knowledge a kind of assurance which surpasses mere logical certainty, nay—to vary a famous saying in a very Socratic sense—"has the power of carrying problems".

This touches a last consideration, the existential character of the whole line of thought. To be sure, there is in question a theoretical problem, clearly stated and accurately treated within its terms. But this problem also includes an existential question: whether the philosopher can be so sure of the truth he has found that he can on the strength of it lead a life so divergent from the views of other men. In more precise terms: whether this particular philosopher, Socrates, who is now speaking and is soon to die, can be sure that he has taught rightly and lived rightly throughout his long life; that his conduct in face of the indictment has been correct; that his death will set the seal on all that he has told his disciples about the philosopher's relation to death. Such a certainty, existential in the strictest sense, can never accrue to him from a mere philosophical perception, nor yet from a merely ethical decision, but only from a religious assurance. How deep this assurance goes, becomes evident as soon as one thinks of the connection between the doctrine of the "Sun" of the Good and that divinity to whom Socrates is conscious of a particular obligation, namely Apollo. In the *Apology* the religious character of the Socratic existence appears especially in the passage where he speaks of the connection of his philosophical calling with the response of the Delphic Oracle. What he does is a service under Apollo, the god of the material and intellectual light of the world. The *Phaedo* also speaks of this service, and with a most personal interest. The connection of the symbol of the Good with the god of the sun and of intellectual light is more than external allegory. It is in the nature of the Socratic-Platonic mind, in all its search after the essential, not to sever religious ideas from the divine figures of tradition; its philosophical statements grow up rather out of the heritage of religious experience and ideas, so that this heritage makes itself heard in them. It is very significant that the conception which gives to Platonic thought its final completion, namely the Idea of the Good, is so intimately bound up with the name of Apollo, and that Socrates so emphatically professes himself to be Apollo's servant.

At the same time it should not be forgotten for a moment that the term in which Socrates-Plato finds the last expression of his religious will, namely the Good, attains to givenness in the Idea. The Idea is related to all sides of human and mundane reality; but the emphasis is on knowledge. In Plato's world the aesthetic moment plays a large part—though it must be added at once that the modern concept does not suffice to express what he understands by the Beautiful: namely the character of that which has turned out well, is truly formed and has attained to valid shape, simply as such. Very pronounced, too, in his world is the concern with what is costly and noble; the craving for that perfection which reveals itself in the shape of the Beautiful, as expressed in the doctrine of Eros—for Eros as centre of action, force, movement, forms the analogy to the objective might of the Good—and much more to this effect might be said. In spite of that it must never be forgotten that this world is that of the philosopher, and receives its characteristic determination through the relation to truth. The Idea is in a decisive manner the expression of truth; so too the religious element, which gives the philosopher the final assurance, is decisively related to truth. In the experience of truth Socrates becomes certain of the meaning of his own existence and of existence in general. The Socratic-Platonic philosophy is anything rather than a mere work of concepts, drawing its life only from the excitement of thought and knowledge; the man behind it is rich, strong, developed all round, and in touch with the most creative culture known to history. Yet the ultimate determinant lies in the wonderful passion for knowledge which fills it. The Platonic man wants to know, at any cost—or, to put it more accurately, at the highest and most vital cost. The expression of this is the doctrine of the philosopher's relation to death; the witness to it the figure and death of Socrates himself. This will for knowledge is as prudent as it is resolute, as conscientious as it is bold. He knows how difficult are the problems, and how hard the limitations, but is convinced that there is such a thing as real, pure knowledge, knowledge which leads to the true certainty. It is this youth-strong will for truth, attacking the problems with such splendid organs of vision and thought, which makes Plato's works immortal. And it is truth in the fullest sense which concerns him; as majesty pure and simple, which cannot be subordinated to any end—but which, as soon as it is willed for the simple reason that it is truth, becomes at once the most fruitful of life-forces.

The closing words of the argument show how little question there is of a "proof" in the strict sense of the word, but rather of a *logos* which interprets experience and brings the mind's life into action.

> *Then, it seems, when death attacks a man, his mortal part dies, but his immortal part retreats before death, and goes away safe and indestructible.*
>
> *It seems so.*
>
> *Then, Cebes, said he, beyond all question the soul is immortal and imperishable; and our souls will indeed exist in the other world.*
>
> *I, Socrates, he replied, have no more objections to urge; your reasoning has quite satisfied me. If Simmias, or any one else, has anything to say, it would be well for him to say it now; for I know not to what other season he can defer the discussion, if he wants to say or to hear anything touching this matter.*
>
> *No, indeed, said Simmias; neither have I any further ground for doubt after what you have said. Yet I cannot help feeling some doubts still in my mind; for the subject of our conversation is a vast one, and I distrust the feebleness of man.*
>
> *You are right, Simmias, said Socrates, and more than that, you must re-examine our original assumptions, however certain they seem to you; and when you have analysed them sufficiently, you will, I think, follow the argument, as far as man can follow it; and when that becomes clear to you, you will seek for nothing more.*
>
> *That is true, he said.*

The next sentences give a practical application to the argument:

> *But then, my friends, said he, we must think of this. If it be true that the soul is immortal, we have to take care of her, not merely on account of the time which we call life, but also on account of all time. Now we can see how terrible is the danger of neglect. For if death had been a release from all things, it would have been a godsend to the wicked; for when they died they would have been released with their souls from the body and from their own wickedness. But now we have found that the soul is immortal; and so her only refuge and salvation from evil is to become as perfect and wise*

as possible. For she takes nothing with her to the other world but her education and culture; and these, it is said, are of the greatest service or of the greatest injury to the dead man, at the very beginning of his journey thither.

THE MYTH CONCERNING THE FATE OF MAN AFTER DEATH

Meaning of the Myths

THE LAST sentence quoted leads up to a description of the world and its various regions, so far as these are co-ordinate with the stages and forms of human life. It is a description of a peculiar kind, with echoes from mythology.

Myths are made up of primitive figures and events; of gods and their doings and fates, in which life is represented poetically. They are not allegories of reality, but reality itself interpreted. One who knows them—taking the word in the old sense of being in and possessing—has knowledge of essence and occurrence, being and meaning. The myths tell how a man must behave and act if life is to be kept in order; they are the forms of right living. The sense of the myth is analogous to that of the Idea. The latter makes the world clear to theoretical, that is, contemplative knowledge; it elevates reality to truth. The myth makes that reality practicable and familiar for life; it teaches wisdom and right action. Not by arguments and precepts, but, as we have said, by figures and events which contain the essence of the life-process itself. The proper place of the myth is in religious worship. Religious words and actions accomplish it, announce it and assume the worshippers into it. Idea and myth thus belong together. The former lights up the dulness of the merely present till it becomes truth; the latter overcomes the confusion of events, enables them to be understood as a divinely significant process, and allows life to find its order therein.

The description of the world as given by Plato at the end of the dialogue is not a myth in the full sense. For one thing, because it does not narrate any event. For myths narrate events which have happened "once upon a time"—in that long ago which denotes no definite point of time, but the horizon to time in general, and so to any period or point in time. But apart from this, Plato's description lacks that primitive note which proclaims that life is here seen and lived directly in figures and events. More strictly speaking, this note has become only an echo; though it is still strong enough to produce a unity of symbol and meaning, an interpretation of existence and a preparation for life's way, which place it after all in close proximity to myth. Plato himself is conscious of this, for he makes Socrates say at the close of his description:

> *A man of sense will not insist that these things are exactly as I have described them. But I think that he will believe that something of the kind is true of the soul and her habitations, seeing that she is shown to be immortal, and that it is worth his while to stake everything on this belief. The venture is a fair one, and he must charm his doubts with spells like these. That is why I have been prolonging the fable all this time.*

Socrates's purpose is to describe the structure of the world; not in the sense of a geography or cosmology, but in such a way that the various regions of the world appear as habitations and at the same time expressions of human life, containing this life and at the same time being constituted by it. The reader must take what is said, then, not as simple description, nor yet as a mere objectivation of psychical states, but must see the objective setting and the life-element as interdependent data.[1] The saying "for what is within is without", with its converse "for what is without is within", is true here in the strictest sense. The geographical and cosmic landscape with its formations is the expression of the inner human scene with its decisions and fates, so that the man who is cognate with it beholds himself in it. Conversely it is that which is imposed on him and brings him always into the state which corresponds to his dispositions and spiritual actuality.

---

[1] The most striking instance of such existential landscape-painting of post-mythical inspiration is Dante's *Divine Comedy*.

The Picture of Existence

To understand the structure of the world described, and especially to explain what is the real point of it, is not altogether easy. But once one has worked through it, the picture displays itself large and simple to the inward eye.

The universe is spherical in shape—a reflection of Greek feeling, which esteemed the neatly formed more than the boundless and immense. In the middle of it is suspended the earth, likewise spherical. It needs no support, not even that of the air, for the equilibrium of cosmic forces, those of the surrounding heaven as well as those of its own structure, hold it in suspense. If we take into account what is further said of it, it must be conceived as very large, larger perhaps than it is in fact. Its surface is pitted by gigantic basins or valleys, which are filled with air, clouds, and in short with everything that we call atmosphere. Such a basin is formed, for example, by the Mediterranean Sea and its surrounding countries, that is, the Greek *oikoumenê*; it is so large that its inhabitants have obviously never set eyes on the enclosing walls. Depressions of a similar kind and of greater or smaller dimensions, deeper or shallower, are scattered over the face of the earth. They contain plains, mountains, seas, rivers, the whole living-space of mankind. So men live, strictly speaking, not on, but in the earth.

The true surface of the earth would only be reached if a man should succeed in reaching and climbing the walls of these depressions. As the air fills only the depressions, he would on completing his ascent leave the atmosphere behind, and, as other men stand by the sea's edge, so he would now stand by the air's edge, while he himself would be in celestial space, which is pervaded by the ether. Thus there are three space-filling fluids. In the depressions is the air with its movements, obscurities and unrest; within the sea of air there is a yet lower depth which is filled with water and consists of the various rivers, lakes and seas; and finally the space above the true surface of the earth contains the pure light-element, the ether.

There too are plains, mountains and growth of every kind. Over it move the heavenly bodies, "still visible in their true shape", which latter is in the lower region of the earth concealed and distorted by the atmosphere. On the heights dwell the perfect, who have overcome the trial of death. They too possess cities and temples; in the temples, however, are not merely the images of the gods, but the gods themselves, and men have intercourse with them.

As on the upper side the celestial region joins that of the inner earth, so on the lower side of the latter the subterranean region. The way to this is through the water. The waters of the different depressions are in communication with one another and with the interior of the earth, where they collect in immense volume. An oscillating movement of the earth's interior, about the origin of which nothing is said, drives them out into the rivers and seas and draws them back again into the depths. Among the rivers four are of special importance. First, the Oceanus, the source of the seas known to the Greeks; then, on the opposite side of the globe, the Acheron, which after a long course sinks into the earth's interior and there flows into the Acherusian Lake; next, the Pyriphlegethon, which rises between the two former and shortly falls into a space filled with fire inside the earth, where it forms a sea of boiling and muddy water; it is this river too which carries along with it the molten lava and sends it up through the volcanoes; lastly, the Cocytus, which receives the water of the Stygian Lake and thereupon plunges likewise into the inside of the earth.

The scenery of these rivers and lakes comprises everything mighty and fearful that experience and fancy surmise in the earth's interior, and forms the sinister region of Tartarus. Here, guided by their guardian spirits, arrive and are judged the souls of the dead. Those who "on account of the greatness of their crimes are judged irremediable", sink to the lowest depth of Tartarus, "whence they never more come forth" (113e). They cannot therefore re-enter the cycle of reincarnation, but are struck out of existence. It is otherwise with those whose moral state can be renewed by virtue of an inner core of good. After the judgment they are thrown into the waters of Cocytus, where they suffer fearful torment. But at the end of every year they come to the shore of the Acherusian Lake and invoke those against whom they have formerly transgressed. If these forgive them, the punishment then ends; otherwise they must continue their expiation. Eventually however—so we may probably interpret the vague description—they reach the abode of the blessed, which has already been mentioned.

Finally, those "who are found to have led exceptionally holy lives" (114b), ascend to the region above the earth and live there in converse with the gods. It may be presumed that they contemplate the Ideas, until their time comes to return to historical existence in a new incarnation and to bring with them thither the hidden memory of essential truth. Among these also are certain souls who do not return, but are finally transported, this time to a region of ultimate fruition—namely those "who have been completely purified by philosophy". They "proceed to dwellings still fairer than these, which are not easily described, and of which I have not time to speak now". Evidently the abode of the Good Itself is meant. There "they live without bodies for all future time" (114c).

The description of these regions and states is uncertain in detail, nor should it be made unduly precise by interpretation. We are dealing with words which still have about them something of the mythical message of "myth-sagas", spells which a man "sings to himself" to give him helping and comforting knowledge. In these pictures Socrates's teaching about mortal and immortal life acquires cosmic shape. Men go to their death with that "education and training" which they have acquired during life. If they have given themselves over to their senses and impulses, their guardian spirit leads them to Tartarus. The disorder in which they find themselves must be set right; this is done by the sentence of the Judge of souls. Those of them who have become thoroughly enslaved to evil are engulfed by a transcendent extreme of evil and so removed from the realm of existence. Nothing further is told us about the nature of this transcendent; it forms the evil Nowhere. Those souls however "who are found to have lived in a middle state (between good and bad)" (113d), undergo purgation. The wavering images of the subterranean streams and lakes with their horror represent the state of conflict and misery of these souls. A beautiful thought makes the men against whom the penitents have offended become present in some mysterious fashion and after each year (the rhythmical unit of time) decide whether the punishment is sufficient. Thus their condition is inserted into the personal relations of society and finally determined thereby.

The region above the earth is the place of spirit, light, truth, the realm of the Ideas. Thither come those men who on earth have led a life according to the spirit. It is not clear from the description whether they too have to undergo a judgment, or whether their inward state simply becomes evident at death, so that their existence requires no further definition (113d). Their life bears henceforth the character of light and truth. To the same region and life those souls also ascend who have been purified by their punishment in Tartarus and have obtained the forgiveness of those whom they have wronged. From there also leads a way to a transcendent extreme, in this case a positive one. Into this place are taken up those who on earth have attained to perfect purity, those who have practised "philosophy" in the true sense. These also return no more to the rhythms of existence. The corporeal has become so foreign to them that they are incapable of any further reincarnation. If the region above the air signifies the realm of the Ideas, we may understand the final transcendence as the region of pure Goodness, the ultimate mystery of light. To "disclose" fuller particulars about it is impossible, says the speaker to Simmias, in mysteriously veiled words; but even what has been set forth is itself magnificent, and "noble is the prize, and great the hope" (114c). Those who live in the region of the Ideas are destined to return to earth at the appointed time and to bring with them, in the hidden memory of their soul, the truth they have beheld.

THE CLOSING SCENE

You, Simmias and Cebes, and the rest will set forth at some future day, each at his own time. But me now, as a tragic poet would say, fate calls at once; and it is time for me to betake myself to the bath. I think that I had better bathe before I drink the poison, and not give the women the trouble of washing my dead body.

Thus begins the final scene in the account of Socrates's death—relieving the gravity of the moment with a delicate self-banter. The narrative, without further comment, shall bring this work to a close.

When he had finished speaking Crito said, Be it so, Socrates. But have you any commands for your friends or for me about your children, or about other things? How shall we serve you best?

Simply by doing what I always tell you, Crito. Take care of your own selves, and you will serve me and mine and yourselves in all that you do, even though you make no promises now. But if you are careless of your own selves, and will not follow the path of life which we have pointed out in our discussions both to-day and at other times, all your promises now, however profuse and earnest they are, will be of no avail.

We will do our best, said Crito. But how shall we bury you?

As you please, he answered; only you must catch me first, and not let me escape you. And then he looked at us with a smile and said, My friends, I cannot convince Crito that I am the Socrates who has been conversing with you, and arranging his arguments in order. He thinks that I am the body which he will presently see a corpse, and he asks how he is to bury me. All the arguments which I have used to prove that I shall not remain with you after I have drunk the poison, but that I shall go away to the happiness of the blessed, with which I tried to comfort you and myself, have been thrown away on him. Do you therefore be my sureties to him, as he was my surety at the trial, but in a different way. He was surety for me then that I would remain; but you must be my sureties to him that I shall go away when I am dead, and not remain with you: then he will feel my death less; and when he sees my body being burnt or buried, he will not be grieved because he thinks that I am suffering dreadful things: and at my funeral he will not say that it is Socrates whom he is laying out, or bearing to the grave, or burying. For, dear Crito, he continued, you must know that to use words wrongly is not only a fault in itself; it also creates evil in the soul. You must be of good cheer, and say that you are burying my body: and you must bury it as you please, and as you think right.

With these words he rose and went into another room to bathe himself: Crito went with him and told us to wait. So we waited, talking of the argument, and discussing it, and then again dwelling on the greatness of the calamity which had fallen upon us: it seemed as if we were going to lose a father, and to be orphans for the rest of our life. When he had bathed, and his children had been brought to him,—he had two sons quite little, and one grown up,—and the women of his family were come, he spoke with them in Crito's presence, and gave them his last commands; then he sent the women and children away, and returned to us. By that time it was near the hour of sunset, for he had been a long while within. When he came back to us from the bath he sat down, but not much was said after that. Presently the servant of the Eleven came and stood before him and said, "I know that I shall not find you unreasonable like other men, Socrates. They are angry with me and curse me when I bid them drink the poison because the authorities make me do it. But I have found you all along the noblest and gentlest and best man that has ever come here; and now I am sure that you will not be angry with me, but with those who you know are to blame. And so farewell, and try to bear what must be as lightly as you can; you know why I have come." With that he turned away weeping, and went out.

Socrates looked up at him, and replied, Farewell: I will do as you say. Then he turned to us and said, How courteous the man is! And the whole time that I have been here, he has constantly come in to see me, and sometimes he has talked to me, and has been the best of men; and now, how generously he weeps for me! Come, Crito, let us obey him: let the poison be brought if it is ready; and if it is not ready, let it be prepared.

Crito replied: Nay, Socrates, I think that the sun is still upon the hills; it has not set. Besides, I know that other men take the poison quite late, and eat and drink heartily, and even enjoy the company of their chosen friends, after the announcement has been made. So do not hurry; there is still time.

Socrates replied: And those whom you speak of, Crito, naturally do so; for they think that they will be gainers by so doing. And I naturally shall not do so; for I think that I should gain nothing by drinking the poison a little later, but my own contempt for so greedily saving up a life which is already spent. So do not refuse to do as I say.

Then Crito made a sign to his slave who was standing by; and the slave went out, and after some delay returned with the man who was to give the poison, carrying it prepared in a cup. When Socrates saw him, he asked, You understand these things, my good sir, what have I to do?

You have only to drink this, he replied, and to walk about until your legs feel heavy, and then lie down; and it will act of itself. With that he handed the cup to Socrates, who took it quite cheerfully, Echecrates, without trembling, and without any change of colour or of feature, and looked up at the man with that fixed glance of his, and asked, What say you to making a libation from this draught? May I, or not? We only prepare so much as we think sufficient, Socrates, he answered. I understand, said Socrates. But I suppose that I may, and must, pray to the gods that my journey hence may be prosperous: that is my prayer; be it so. With these words he put the cup to his lips and drank the poison quite calmly and cheerfully. Till then most of us had been able to control our grief fairly well; but when we saw him drinking, and then the poison finished, we could do so no longer: my tears came fast in spite of myself, and I covered my face and wept for myself: it was not for him, but at my own misfortune in losing such a friend. Even before that Crito had been unable to restrain his tears, and had gone away; and Apollodorus, who had never once ceased weeping the whole time, burst into a loud cry, and made us one and all break down by his sobbing and grief, except only Socrates himself. What are you doing, my friends? he exclaimed. I sent away the women chiefly in order that they might not offend in this way; for I have heard that a man should die in silence. So calm yourselves and bear up. When we heard that we were ashamed, and we ceased from weeping. But he walked about, until he said that his legs were getting heavy, and then he lay down on his back, as he was told. And the man who gave the poison began to examine his feet and legs, from time to time: then he pressed his foot hard, and asked if there was any feeling in it; and Socrates said, No: and then his legs, and so higher and higher, and showed us that he was cold and stiff. And Socrates felt himself, and said that when it came to his heart, he should be gone. He was already growing cold about the groin, when he uncovered his face, which had been covered, and spoke for the last time. Crito, he said, I owe a cock to Asclepius; do not forget to pay it. It shall be done, replied

Crito. Is there anything else that you wish? He made no answer to this question; but after a short interval there was a movement, and the man uncovered him, and his eyes were fixed. Then Crito closed his mouth and his eyes.

Such was the end, Echecrates, of our friend, a man, I think, who was the wisest and justest, and the best man that I have ever known.

www.ingramcontent.com/pod-product-compliance
Lightning Source LLC
Chambersburg PA
CBHW031253230426
43670CB00005B/174